Reading Comprehension

Grade 1

Printed in the U.S.A.

ISBN 978-0-544-26765-7

2 3 4 5 6 7 8 9 10   0928   22 21 20 19 18 17 16 15 14

4500493590   A B C D E F G

Dear Parent,

Welcome to the *Core Skills Reading Comprehension* series! You have selected a unique book that focuses on developing your child's comprehension skills, the reading and thinking processes associated with the printed word. Because this series was designed by experienced reading professionals, your child will have reading success as well as gain a firm understanding of the necessary skills outlined in the Common Core State Standards.

Reading should be a fun, relaxed activity for children. They should read selections that relate to or build on their own experiences. Vocabulary should be presented in a sequential and logical progression. The selections in this series build on these philosophies to insure your child's reading success. Other important features in this series that will further aid your child include:

- Short reading selections of interest to a young reader.

- Vocabulary introduced in context and repeated often.

- Comprehension skills applied in context to make the reading more relevant.

- Multiple-choice exercises that develop skills for standardized test taking.

You may wish to have your child read the selections silently or orally, but you will find that sharing the selections and activities with your child will provide additional confidence and support to succeed. When learners experience success, learning becomes a continuous process moving them onward to higher achievements. Moreover, the more your child reads, the more proficient she or he will become.

Enjoy this special time with your child!

Sincerely,
The Educators and Staff of
Houghton Mifflin Harcourt

Core Skills Reading Comprehension
GRADE 1

Table of Contents

© Houghton Mifflin Harcourt Publishing Company

Table of Contents
Core Skills Reading Comprehension, Grade 1

Skills Correlation

LANGUAGE ARTS SKILL	SELECTION
COMPREHENSION	
Literary Texts	
*Answer Questions About Key Details	6, 14, 15, 16, 18, 19, 21, 22, 24, 26, Skills Review: Selections 22–26, 27, 28, 29, 30, 31, 32
*Retelling Stories	22
*Characters, Setting, Plot	2, 4, 6, 14, 15, 16, 19, 21, 22, 24, 26, 27, 28, 29, 30, 31, 32
*Emotion and Sensory Words	18
*Compare Fiction and Nonfiction	19
*Narrator	21
*Illustrations in Literary Texts	22
*Compare and Contrast Characters' Adventures and Experiences in Stories	14 and 15
Drawing Conclusions	14, Skills Review: Selections 14–16, 26
Perceiving Relationships	16, 22
Make Judgments	24, 30
Cause and Effect	15
Predicting Outcomes	16
Sentence Comprehension	1, 2, 4, 27, 28, 31, 32
Sequencing	15, Skills Review: Selections 14–16, 18, 19, 21, Skills Review: Selections 17–21, 26, Skills Review: Selections 22–26
Informational Texts	
*Answer Questions About Details	3, Skills Review: Selections 1–4, 8, 11, 12, 17, 20, 23, 25, 33, 34
*Answer Questions About Main Ideas	7, 11, 20
*Connections	20
*Answer Questions to Determine Word Meaning	33
*Text Features	23, Skills Review: Selections 22–26
*Illustrations in Informational Texts	33
*Supporting Details	19, 23, 25, 33
*Compare and Contrast Texts	34
Drawing Conclusions	5, 7, 8, 10, 23, 33
Perceiving Relationships	9, 10, 23, Skills Review: Selections 27–34
Sentence Comprehension	3, Skills Review: Selections 5–9, 11, 12, Skills Review: Selections 27–34
Sequencing	25

*Aligns to the Common Core State Standards for English Language Arts for grade 1

Skills Correlation, part 2

LANGUAGE ARTS SKILL	SELECTION
VOCABULARY	
*Word Meaning	1, 4, Skills Review: Selections 1–4, 9, 13, Skills Review: Selections 10–13, 14, 15, Skills Review: Selections 14–16, 17, 18, 19, 20, 21, Skills Review: Selections 17–21, 22, 23, 26, Skills Review: Selections 22–26, 27, 28, 29, 30, 31, 32, 33, 34, Skills Review: Selections 27–34
*Words in Context	4, Skills Review: Selections 1–4, 9, 13, Skills Review: Selections 10–13, 14, 15, Skills Review: Selections 14–16, Skills Review: Selections 17–21, 27, 33, 34
*Suffixes	25
*Antonyms	23
*Classifying	5, 6, 13, 17, 21, Skills Review: Selections 17–21, Skills Review: Selections 22–26, 32, Skills Review: Selections 27–34
Picture Clues	1, Skills Review: Selections 10–13, 14, 16
GRAMMAR AND USAGE	
Pronouns	17, 18, 20, Skills Review: Selections 17–21
Punctuation	27, 29, 31, Skills Review: Selections 27–34
Adverbs (*When* and *Where* Phrases)	28, 30, 32, 34, Skills Review: Selections 27–34
RESEARCH AND STUDY SKILL	
Following Directions	22, 24, 25, 26, Skills Review: Selections 22–26, Skills Review: Selections 27–34

*Aligns to the Common Core State Standards for English Language Arts for grade 1

© Houghton Mifflin Harcourt Publishing Company

Vocabulary List

The selections are comprised of words carefully chosen from the Dolch Basic Sight Vocabulary and the Kucera-Francis word list. Words that appear most frequently in primary reading basal series were also used.

This vocabulary list includes the important words in the selections and activities.

Selection 1
a
big
dogs
house
in
little
live
people
see
the
Tags
Wags
walk

Selection 2
an
animal
can
cat
here
is
new
no
not
run
to
yes

Selection 3
children
food
get
home
is
work

Selection 4
are
Dad
Mom
working

Selection 5
bug
eat
for
make
spider

Selection 6
Dan
do
Jill
Nan
what
who
Will

Selection 7
corn
fish
get
go
have
it
out
raccoon
says
tree

Selection 8
ant
eating
hill
into
I
many
take
they
walking
will
you

Selection 9
bee
flower
from
good
something

Selection 10
bird
climb
fly
one
squirrel
two

Selection 11
at
be
duck
frog
its
look
name
pond
water

Selection 12
by
fun
grass
play
swim
too

Selection 13
am
fox

Selection 14
chipmunk
ground
happy
rock
she
want
where

Selection 15
back
comes
door
fast
her
me
snake
so

Selections 14 and 15
different
same

Selection 16
away
cold
good-bye
mud
sleep
Selection
under

Selection 17
father
finger
front
fur
jump
kangaroo
mother
paws
pouch
tail

Selection 18
again
bath
morning
mud
now
puddle
said
think
time
tub
went
wet

Selection 19
day
did
let's
mother
real
talk
this

Selection 20
found
making
nest
oak
were

Selection 21
all
gave
inside
park
some
then

Selection 22
bottom
care
each
evening
every
guess
know
middle
shelf
their

Selection 23
careful
catch
feet
find
games
land
well

Selection 24
flew
hid
hopped
just
left
pick
quick
worm

Selection 25
last
Monday
other
playground
race
ready
second
started

Selection 26
deep
fence
Friday
lost
please
Saturday
snowed
Thursday
Tuesday
Wednesday

Selection 27
beaks
dropped
never
pretty
spring
surprise
very
window

Selection 28
buttons
his
hunted
lunch
school

Selection 29
around
barked
began
could
cry
sea
seal
smell

Selection 30
funny
jar
jelly
shorter
spots
tadpoles
watched

Selection 31
don't
foxes
grab
near
nothing
wings
wish

Selection 32
bent
crawl
giraffe
lifted
mouth
neck
reach
tiny

Selection 33
desert
cactus
camel
lizard
rabbit

Selection 34
afternoon
bat
daytime
den
night
shade

Vocabulary List

Name _____ Date _____

Selection 1

See the house.

People live in the house.

See the dogs.

See Wags. See Tags.

The people walk.

The people walk in the big house.

Wags walks in a little house.

Tags walks in a little house.

1

Name _____ Date _____

(A) **Draw a circle around the right words. One is done for you.**

1.

dogs   (dog)

4.

big dog   little dog

2.

Tags   house

5.

The dogs walk.
The people walk.

3.

people   house

6.

a little house
a big house

2

Name _____ Date _____

B **Draw a line under the pictures that match each sentence.**

1. People live in houses.

a.

c. 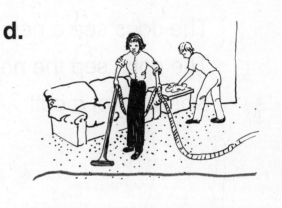 ✓

b.

d.

2. The dogs walk.

a.

c.

b.

d.

Selection 1
Core Skills Reading Comprehension, Grade 1

Selection 2

The dogs see a new house.

The dogs see the new animal.

No! No! Not a cat!

A cat cannot live here! No cat can live here!

See Tags run! See Wags run!

See the cat walk to the house.

Yes, a cat can live here!

4

Name _____ Date _____

A Write ___ yes ___ or ___ no ___.
One is done for you.

1. The dogs can see a new house. ___ yes

2. A cat can live in a house. ___ no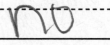

3. A house is an animal. ___ no

4. Dogs can run. ___ yes

5. A house can run. ___ no

6. The dogs see a new animal. ___ yes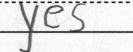

7. A house can walk. ___ no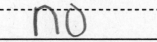

5

Name _____ Date _____

B **Draw a circle around the sentence that matches the picture.**

1.
   Here is a little animal.

   Here is a big animal.

2.
   Animals run here.

   Animals walk here.

3.
   See people in a house.

   See people here.

4.
   Here is a new dog.

   Here is a new cat.

5.
   See the doghouse walk.

   A dog is in the house.

6.
   No cat is here.

   A cat is here.

Selection 3

See the house.

The house is a home.

People live in the house.

People live here.

See the children.

The children work.

The children get food.

The children work here.

7

A **Draw a line under the ones who are working.**

1.

2.

3.

4.

5.

6.

8

Name _____ Date _____

B Draw a circle around the sentence that matches the picture.

1.

Children get food.

Children live here.

2.

People live here.

Here is food.

3.

See a house.

Here is food.

4.

Children see food.

The house works.

5.

The people live here.

The people work here.

6.

People get food.

Here is a house.

Selection 3
Core Skills Reading Comprehension, Grade 1

Selection 4

Here is Dad.

Dad works here.

Dad works to get food.

See Mom.

Mom is working.

Mom works to get food.

See the children.

The children are here.

The children are working.

10

Name _____ Date _____

 A **Write the best word to finish the sentence.**

1. Mom and Dad are (live, people). ___ **people** ___

2. Mom works to get (not, food). _____

3. People (food, work). _____

4. Children are in the
   (people, house). _____

5. Here are the (homes, is). _____

6. The people are (working, get). _____

7. The children live (food, here). _____

Selection 4
Core Skills Reading Comprehension, Grade 1

B **Draw a circle around the picture that matches the sentence. One is done for you.**

1. Here is Mom working.

a.    b.

2. Dad and the children are here.

a.    b.

3. The people get food.

a.    b.

4. Children live here.

a.    b.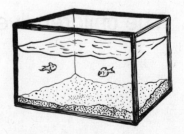

12

Skills Review: Selections 1–4

(A) **Draw a circle around the right words.**

1.

not new   new

2.

not new   new

3.

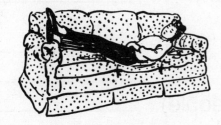

is working

is not working

4.

cannot get food

can get food

5.

The house is new.

The house is not new.

6.

People live here.

People work here.

Name _____ Date _____

B Write the best word to finish the sentence.

1. See the children (not, walk). _____

2. The people get a new (home, here). _____

3. Can the children live (here, house)? _____

4. The house is (new, not). _____

5. Dad and Mom get (new, food). _____

6. The children are (working, can). _____

7. Dad and Mom are (house, people). _____

Selection 5

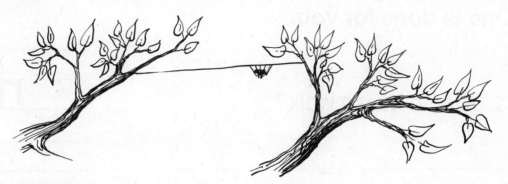

Here is a spider.

The spider can work.

The spider can make a new house.

See the new home.

Bugs see the new home.

Bugs walk in the new house.

The spider can get food.

The spider eats a bug.

Name _____ Date _____

 A **Read each question. Write <u>yes</u> or <u>no</u>.**
One is done for you.

1. Can a house walk?

                                                    no

2. Can a spider eat bugs?

3. Can people walk?

4. Can children eat?

5. Can a house work for food?

6. Can a spider make a new home?

7. Can a spider walk?

Name _____ Date _____

B **Read the words. Match the picture to the right word.**
One is done for you.

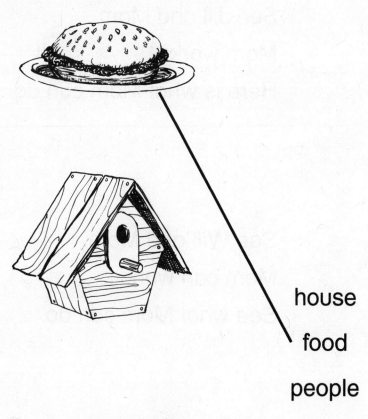

house

food

people

17

See Jill and Mom.

Mom works.

Here is what Mom can do.

See Will and Mom.

Mom can work.

See what Mom can do.

Here are Nan and Dad.

See Dad work.

Dad works and works.

See Dan and Dad.

Dad is working.

Dad works here.

Name _Farah_   Date _____

A **Who? What? Draw a line under the right one.**

1. Who can make a house?

2. What cannot walk?

3. Who can eat?

home   Dad   live

4. What lives here?

Dad   see   spider

5. Who can walk?

food   Mom   new

6. Who are people?

a house   children and Dad   walk and walk

7. Who can get a new house?

Mom and Dad   live and eat   food and work

8. What cannot eat?

house   children   people

19

Name _____ Date _____

B **Read the words. Put an X on the people.**

Dan	Will	houses	not
walk	Mom	live	Dad
for	home	Nan	is
children	eat	food	get
do	new	Jill	in

C **Draw a circle around the right words.**

1.

cannot walk

can eat

3.

works in a house

can eat

2.

can make food

are in a house

4.

is not new

is new

20

Selection 7

See the tree.

The tree is a home.

What can live in the house?

See what lives here.

It is for a raccoon.

Raccoons can live in trees.

The raccoon can go in.

It can go out to get food.

It gets corn and fish to eat.

Name _____ Date _____

A **Draw a line under the best name for this selection.**

    1. A House for a Fish

    2. The Raccoon's Home

    3. The Tree's Food

B **Read each selection. Draw a line under the best name for the selection.**

Will gets a fish to eat.
The raccoon sees Will.
It walks to Will.
Will says, "No, Raccoon!
The fish is for people."

    1. The Raccoon Gets Food

        Will Eats the Raccoon

        Food for People

Dad Raccoon says, "Walk in!
Here is corn.
Eat and eat.
No people are here."

    2. The People Eat Food

        The Raccoons Get Food

        The Raccoons Get Fish

© Houghton Mifflin Harcourt Publishing Company

Name _____ Date _____

C Read each sentence. Write <u>yes</u> or <u>no</u>.

1. A tree can have fish in it.

   _____

2. Raccoons can get a new home.

   _____

3. Corn is food for raccoons.

   _____

4. Jill can eat corn and fish.

   _____

5. Trees can eat raccoons.

   _____

6. A fish can eat.

   _____

7. Corn can walk to a tree.

   _____

23

Selection 8

Can you see a house here?

Yes, the hill is a home.

It is a home for bugs.

The little bugs are ants.

Many ants live in the house.

Many ants work in the hill.

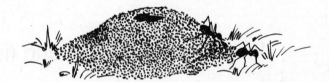

Ants walk in and out.

They go out to get food.

They take food into the hill.

Name _____ Date _____

A **What do you see? Draw a circle around the right ones.**
There are 2 right ones for each picture.

1. See a raccoon walk.
2. They eat corn.
3. They eat fish.
4. Here are 2 raccoons.

1. Many ants are working.
2. Many ants are in the house.
3. Many ants are walking.
4. The ants are eating corn.

1. I see children here.
2. Children eat fish.
3. Here are many fish.
4. Here are many children.

1. Children take corn.
2. They eat ants.
3. A raccoon takes a fish.
4. The raccoon will eat fish.

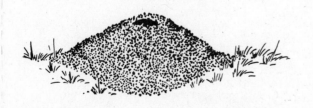

1. Raccoons live here.
2. Ants eat raccoons.
3. Ants live here.
4. Ants work here.

25

Name _____ Date _____

B Read each question. Write yes or no.

1. Do hills eat corn?   _____

2. Are ants little?   _____

3. Do many ants live in hills?   _____

4. Do spiders live in little hills?   _____

5. Do trees walk to ants?   _____

6. Do many people work to get food?   _____

7. Do trees eat raccoons?   _____

Selection 9

What lives here?

Can children live here? No.

It is a home for bees.

Many bees live here.

Many bees work here.

They go to the flowers.

They take something from the flowers.

Bees take something into the house.

They make food from it.

The food is good to eat.

People will eat what the bees make.

What food do bees make?

A **Can they get home? Draw a line to the right home.**

1.    

2.   

3.   

4.    

5.    

Name _____ Date _____

B **Write the best word to finish the sentence.**

1. Bees go to the (from, flowers).

2. From flowers bees get (something, see).

3. Bees take something (home, have).

4. Bees make (flowers, food).

5. The food is (go, good).

6. People will eat (it, is).

7. Corn is something to (it, eat).

Selection 9
Core Skills Reading Comprehension, Grade 1

Skills Review: Selections 5–9

A **Who? What? Draw a line under the right one.**

1. What can take a walk?

  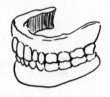

2. What can make something?

3. What cannot eat?

raccoons   hills   bees

4. What can people do?

make a new ant

make a new house

make a new raccoon

5. Who are **not** people?

Nan and Dan

bugs and flowers

many children

Name _____ Date _____

B **Read each selection. Draw a circle around a good name for it.**

Raccoons eat corn and fish.
Ants eat many foods.
Fish eat bugs.

1. Who Can Walk?

2. What Animals Eat

3. What Bugs Eat

The children take a walk.
They go to the flowers.
They get many flowers.
They take the flowers to Mom.

1. The Flowers Walk

2. Mom Takes a Walk

3. Something for Mom

Name _____ Date _____

C **What do you see? Draw a circle around the right ones.**
There are 2 right ones for each picture.

1. Raccoons live in the flowers.

2. Bees take something from flowers.

3. Bees work here.

4. The bees make a home.

1. Dan gets something new.

2. Dan gets something to eat.

3. Dan sees something new here.

4. Dan takes a walk.

Selection 10

The tree is a home.

It is a house.

See what lives here.

Here is the squirrel's home.

One squirrel lives here.

The squirrel climbs the tree.

Two birds live here.

They fly home.

What lives here?

Bugs live here.

Little bugs climb the tree.

Name _____ Date _____

A **What is at home here? Write the words in the correct spaces. Use these words.**

squirrel   raccoon   children   bird   people

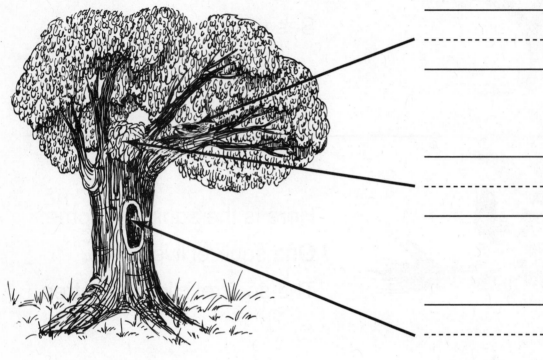

_____

- - - - - - - - - - - - - - - - - - - -

_____

_____

- - - - - - - - - - - - - - - - - - - -

_____

_____

- - - - - - - - - - - - - - - - - - - -

_____

_____

- - - - - - - - - - - - - - - - - - - -

_____

_____

- - - - - - - - - - - - - - - - - - - -

_____

34

Name _____ Date _____

B Read each question. Circle <u>yes</u> or <u>no</u>.

1. Can a squirrel climb?   yes   no

2. Can trees fly?   yes   no

3. Can two flowers make a house?   yes   no

4. Can two little children climb trees?   yes   no

5. Can one raccoon live in a tree?   yes   no

6. Can one squirrel take a walk?   yes   no

7. Can fish live in hills?   yes   no

8. Do bugs climb?   yes   no

9. Do hills fly?   yes   no

10. Is corn something to eat?   yes   no

35

Selection 11

Here is a pond.

What can be in a pond?

Many animals can live here.

Ducks live here.

The ducks look for food.

They look in the water.

See the duck!

Look at its food.

Fish live in water.

Little fish can be food
for ducks.

What can be in the pond?

bugs   frogs   flowers

Name _____ Date _____

 A **Which one is right? Put a ✔ by it. One is done for you.**

1. What is a good name for this selection?

_____ **a.** Water in the House

_____ **b.** People in the Pond

__✔__ **c.** Animals in the Pond

2. What is **not** in this selection?

_____ **a.** a duck eating

_____ **b.** what a bug eats

_____ **c.** water in a pond

3. What animals can live in water?

_____ **a.** people

_____ **b.** frogs

_____ **c.** squirrels

4. What do ducks do in the water?

_____ **a.** climb trees

_____ **b.** take a walk

_____ **c.** look for food

5. What can eat fish?

_____ **a.** people, raccoons, and ducks

_____ **b.** ducks, ponds, and trees

_____ **c.** flowers, trees, and houses

37

Name _____ Date _____

B **Look at the pictures. Read the sentences. Match each picture to the best sentence.**

1.

a. The frog is not in the pond.

b. Two people play in the water.

2.

c. The bug can fly.

3.

d. The fish eats the flower.

4.

e. It looks for something to eat.

Selection 11
Core Skills Reading Comprehension, Grade 1

Selection 12

Many animals live in ponds.

They have to swim.

See the grass by the pond.

Animals can live in the grass.

Frogs live in the pond.

They go into the grass, too.

Ducks can be in the grass.

They can go into the water, too.

Many animals play in the water.

Many animals play by the water.

They have fun.

39

Name _____ Date _____

A **Read each sentence. Draw a line under the correct picture. One is done for you.**

1. Mom can swim.

a.    b.

2. I have fun.

a.    b.

3. Children play by a tree.

a.    b.

4. Bees fly home.

a.   b.

5. Fish can live here.

a.    b.

40

B **Who? What? Draw a circle around the right one.**

1. Who lives in a hill?

   are   ant   out

2. Who will eat a bug?

   be   by   bird

3. What is something to eat?

   can   corn   climb

4. Who can live in water?

   Dad   duck   do

5. Who gets something from flowers?

   bee   be   by

6. Who can have fun?

   play   pond   people

7. Who can have a home?

   are   ant   out

Selection 13

The bug says, "Look! I am big."

The bird says, "No! **I** am big.

You are little."

The bird says, "I am little."

The fox says, "Yes, you are little.

I am big."

Dad says, "Look here, Fox.

I am big.

You are the little one."

The fox says, "I can look.

I can see you.

You are the big one."

42

A **Draw a line from each sentence to the correct picture.**
One is done for you.

a.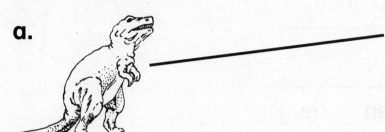

1. I am big.

b.

2. I am little.

a.

3. It is something little.

b.

4. It is something big.

a.

5. See the little one.

b.

6. See the big one.

43

Name _____ Date _____

B **Write the best word to finish the sentence.**

1. The bird looks for food.

   _____

   It will eat _____.

   children   bugs

2. Here is something good to eat.

   _____

   People will eat _____.

   fish   fly

3. A fox will climb.

   _____

   It can climb a _____.

   hill   pond

4. Animals can have fun.

   _____

   They will _____.

   play   pond

5. The frogs have fun in the water.

   _____

   They will _____.

   swim   fly

44

Name _____ Date _____

Skills Review: Selections 10–13

A Write the name of each thing in the picture.
Use these words.

grass   fish   duck
raccoon   flower   frog

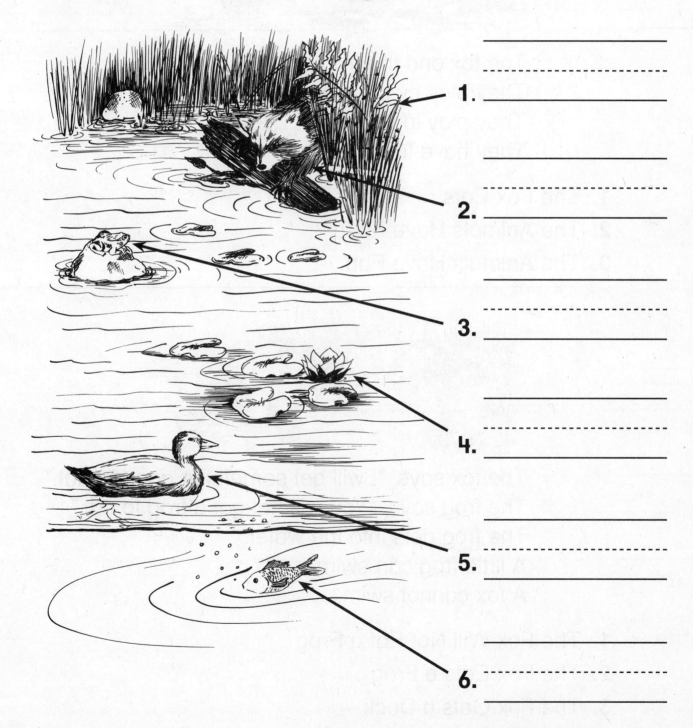

1. _____

2. _____

3. _____

4. _____

5. _____

6. _____

45

Name _____ Date _____

B **Read each selection. Draw a circle around a good name for it.**

The fox and the frog play.
They play by the water.
They play in the grass.
They have fun.

1. The Fox Eats
2. The Animals Have Food
3. The Animals Have Fun

The fox says, "I will get something good to eat."
The frog says, "You will not get a frog to eat."
The frog gets into the water.
A little frog can swim.
A fox cannot swim.

1. The Fox Will Not Eat a Frog
2. The Fox Eats a Frog
3. The Fox Gets a Duck

Skills Review: Selections 10–13
Core Skills Reading Comprehension, Grade 1

C **Write the best word to finish the sentence.**

1. Mom will go out to play.

   _____

   -

   Mom will have _____.

   fly   fun

2. Jill has something to eat.

   _____

   -

   Jill has _____.

   corn   climb

3. The flower is little.

   _____

   -

   A flower cannot _____.

   something   swim

4. The spider has a new home.

   _____

   -

   The spider will get many _____.

   hills   bugs

5. Dad has something new.

   _____

   -

   Dad says, "It is for _____."

   you   out

47

Selection 14: Paired

Chipmunk says, "I have a good house.
It is in the ground by the rocks."
A big fox says, "I want to see
where Chipmunk lives."

Chipmunk runs home.
The home is in the ground.

The fox says, "I see where Chipmunk lives.
I want to eat.
I will get into Chipmunk's house."
The fox is not happy.
She says, "I am too big.
I cannot get into the little home."

48

Name _____ Date _____

A **Draw a circle around the best ending for each sentence.**

1. The fox wants to get into the chipmunk's house.
   She wants to

   a. play with the chipmunk.

   b. swim with the chipmunk.

   c. get food.

2. The fox cannot get into the chipmunk's home.
   The fox says,

   a. "I will not eat a duck."

   b. "I will not eat a chipmunk."

   c. "I will eat good rocks."

B **Write the word to finish the sentence. Use these words.**

| fox | lives | run | ground |

_____

1. A chipmunk's house is in the _____.

2. The chipmunk can _____.

3. Here is where the animal _____.

49

© Houghton Mifflin Harcourt Publishing Company

Core Skills Reading Comprehension, Grade 1

Name _____ Date _____

C <u>Underline</u> the words that match the picture.

1.

not on the ground
on the ground

4.

a frog by a bug
a frog by a flower

2.

happy people
happy ducks

5.

on the grass
on the water

3.

the rock
two rocks

6.

is a bird
is not a bird

50

Selection 15: Paired

Chipmunk says, "I am happy.
The fox cannot get me."

Here comes a snake.
She says, "I am not too big.
I will get into Chipmunk's house.
I like to eat little animals."
Chipmunk sees the snake.
She runs back into her house fast.

The snake is fast, too.
She is in Chipmunk's house.

Chipmunk says, "The snake cannot get me!
I have a back door to my house.
The back door is by the rocks."

51

Name _____ Date _____

A Underline the best name for the selection.

    1. Food for a Chipmunk

    2. A Snake in the House

    3. Food for a Fox

B Write the word to finish the sentence. Use these words.

fast	me	rocks	door

    1. A chipmunk runs _____.

    2. She runs out the _____.

    3. The back door is by the _____.

C What comes first in the selection? Write a 1 in the box next to it. What comes next? Write a 2. What comes last? Write a 3.

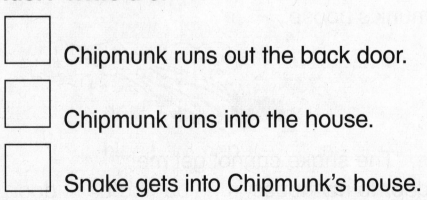

☐ Chipmunk runs out the back door.

☐ Chipmunk runs into the house.

☐ Snake gets into Chipmunk's house.

D **What will come next? Put a ✔ by it. One is done for you.**

1. The snakes have no food.

   _____ **a.** So they are happy.

   ✔ **b.** So they look for something to eat.

   _____ **c.** So they go to live with a spider.

2. The frogs are in the pond.

   _____ **a.** So they will run.

   _____ **b.** So they will walk.

   _____ **c.** So they will swim.

3. The bugs have a home in the tree.

   _____ **a.** So they have to climb.

   _____ **b.** So they have to swim.

   _____ **c.** So they can get a fish.

4. The spider works to make a new house.

   _____ **a.** So she will get bugs to eat.

   _____ **b.** So she will get a bird.

   _____ **c.** So she will live in the anthill.

5. The snake gets into Chipmunk's house.

   _____ **a.** So the snake works with Chipmunk.

   _____ **b.** So the chipmunk and the snake play.

   _____ **c.** So the chipmunk runs out the back door.

E **Think about the two Chipmunk stories. <u>Underline</u> the sentence that answers the question.**

1. How are the fox and the snake different?

   a. The fox cannot get into Chipmunk's house.

   b. The snake cannot get into Chipmunk's house.

   c. The fox does not want to get into Chipmunk's house.

2. How are the fox and the snake the same?

   a. They want to eat Chipmunk.

   b. They want a house.

   c. They live in a tree.

3. How is Chipmunk the same in both stories?

   a. She plays.

   b. She goes home.

   c. She is not happy.

4. What does Chipmunk do in both stories?

   a. She eats.

   b. She swims.

   c. She runs.

Selection 16

The duck says, "It is cold.
You will not see me, dogs.
I will go away. Good-bye."

Tags says, "Where will you go?"
The duck says, "Where it is not cold."

The frog says, "Good-bye, Tags.
Good-bye, Wags.
I will go away, too.
It is too cold."
Wags says, "Where will you go, frog?"

Frog says, "I go under the water here.
I get into the mud.
I will sleep in the mud."

Wags and Tags see the duck fly away.
They see the frog swim away.

Wags and Tags say, "It is cold.
We will go into the people's house."

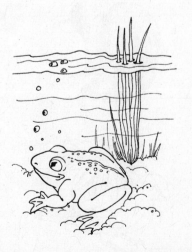

55

Name _____ Date _____

A Draw a circle around the answer to each question.

1. What is this selection about?

   a. Dogs sleep under the water.

   b. A cat is under the flowers.

   c. Animals want to go away.

2. What is not in the selection?

   a. Wags says, "It is cold."

   b. A cat sleeps in the mud.

   c. A duck can fly away.

B Where is the bird? Draw a line from the words to the correct picture.

1.

under a flower

4.

on the corn

2.

on a squirrel

5.

on the hill

3.

on a raccoon

6.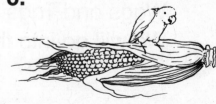

in a spider's home

56

Selection 16
Core Skills Reading Comprehension, Grade 1

C **Make a circle around the answer to each question.**

1. What cannot fly away?

2. What do raccoons eat?

3. Where is something under a tree?

4. What can you climb?

D **Will Wags and Tags ever see their friends again? Tell why.**

Skills Review: Selections 14–16

A **Underline** the sentence that answers the question.
One is done for you.

1. What makes Dan happy?

   a. He has new flowers.

   b. He has a new animal.

2. Where is the bird?

   a. It plays by the tree.

   b. It is in its home.

3. Where is the bee?

   a. It is under the flower.

   b. It is on the flower.

4. Who can sleep?

   a. A door can sleep.

   b. A dog can sleep.

Skills Review: Selections 14–16
Core Skills Reading Comprehension, Grade 1

Name _____ Date _____

Ⓑ Write the best word to answer the question.

1. Where do frogs sleep?

mom   mud   many

_____

2. Where can ducks fly?

away   and   are

_____

3. Who can come out the back door?

rocks   flowers   people

_____

4. What can go fast?

a rock   a snake   ground

_____

5. What cannot be happy?

a door   birds   children

_____

6. Where do ants want to live?

a door   a hill   a pond

_____

7. What do spiders want to eat?

people   rocks   bugs

_____

Name _____ Date _____

C **Write the word to finish the sentence. Use these words.**

ground	want	happy	fast

_____

----

1. People have fun. They are _____.

   _____

   ----

2. She can run _____.

   _____

   ----

3. What do you _____?

D **Underline the best answer.**

1. The bird wants to eat ants.

   a. So the ants have to run fast.

   b. So the ants play with the bird.

   c. So the ants eat the bird.

2. We like to fish.

   a. So we fly into the tree.

   b. So we live by the water.

   c. So we dig in the ground.

E **Read the selection. <u>Underline</u> the best name for the selection.**

The children want something to eat.

They get food they like.

They play and run fast.

They have fun.

1. The Happy People

2. The Happy Rocks

3. By the Door

F **Read the selection below. What comes first? Write a 1 in the box next to it. What comes next? Write a 2. What comes last? Write a 3.**

Dan says, "I do not want a big rock here.

I will take it out."

He gets the rock out.

Dan sees a big snake on the ground.

He runs away to his house.

☐ He runs home fast.

☐ He sees a big snake.

☐ Dan wants the rock out.

Selection 17

This animal has a big tail.

It has big back paws.

It jumps on its back feet.

Its front paws are like hands.

Look at your little finger.

This animal's new baby is that little.

The baby has no fur. It cannot see.

It lives in the mother's pouch.

It lives there a long time.

It gets big in the pouch.

What animal is this?

It is a kangaroo.

Selection 17
Core Skills Reading Comprehension, Grade 1

Name _____   Date _____

 Which one is right? Put a ✔ by it. One is done for you.

1. What has a pouch?

_____ **a.** a new baby

_____ **b.** your hand

__✔__ **c.** the mother animal

2. What animal is this?

_____ **a.** kangaroo

_____ **b.** rabbit

_____ **c.** lion

3. Where must a new baby kangaroo live?

_____ **a.** in an egg

_____ **b.** in the mother's pouch

_____ **c.** in a nest

4. How do these animals jump?

_____ **a.** on four paws

_____ **b.** on three paws

_____ **c.** on two paws

5. What is a good name for this selection?

_____ **a.** A Little Finger

_____ **b.** A Funny Animal

_____ **c.** A Little Bunny

6. What do you know about the new baby?

_____ **a.** It has brown fur.

_____ **b.** It has no back paws.

_____ **c.** It cannot see.

B **Draw lines to match the words.**
One is done for you.

1. a bag

2. not old

3. to jump

4. not the front

5. It is on your hand.

6. an animal's feet

paws

talk

pouch

hop

finger

new

back

C **Write the words in the right place. One is done for you.**

paw   pouch   fur   tail   hop   back   front

1. fur _____

2. _____

3. _____

4. _____

5. _____

6. _____

Selection 17
Core Skills Reading Comprehension, Grade 1

Name _____ Date _____

 Who? What? Circle the right words. One is done for you.

1. <u>Kangaroos</u> are funny animals.

   | She |
   | (They) | jump far.

2. The new <u>baby</u> cannot see.

   | It |
   | They | cannot jump.

3. The <u>mother kangaroo</u> has a pouch.

   | He |
   | She | has a baby in the pouch.

4. The kangaroo's <u>tail</u> is big.

   | She |
   | It | is not little.

5. <u>Father kangaroo</u> lives far away.

   | He |
   | She | can hop fast.

6. Baby <u>kangaroos</u> have no fur.

   | It |
   | They | will get fur soon.

7. The <u>pouch</u> is on the kangaroo.

   | It |
   | They | has a baby in it.

Selection 17
Core Skills Reading Comprehension, Grade 1

Name _____ Date _____

Selection 18

"Bath time now!" said Dan and Jill.

The dogs said, "Not today!"

"No bath again," said Tags and Wags.

"It's time to run away!"

But Jill and Dan were too fast.

The dogs went into the tub.

Off came all the mud that morning.

The dogs got a good rub!

Jill and Dan were happy.

Tags and Wags ran out to play.

They jumped in a big mud puddle.

They were wet for the rest of the day!

A Which one is right? Put a ✔ by it.

1. Who got a bath?

_____ **a.** Dan

_____ **b.** animals

_____ **c.** Jill

2. Where did they get a bath?

_____ **a.** in a bed

_____ **b.** in a tub

_____ **c.** in some mud

3. How do Tags and Wags feel when they hear "Bath time now"?

_____ **a.** happy

_____ **b.** sad

_____ **c.** fast

4. Why did the children put the dogs into the bathtub?

_____ **a.** The dogs wanted a bath.

_____ **b.** The children wanted a bath.

_____ **c.** The children wanted the dogs to look good.

5. What do you think happened to the dogs at the end of the day?

_____ **a.** The children said, "Good dogs!"

_____ **b.** The dogs went into the tub again.

_____ **c.** Jill and Dan jumped in the mud.

6. What is a good name for this poem?

_____ **a.** The Big Bathtub

_____ **b.** Two Dogs in a Tub

_____ **c.** A Little Puddle

Name _____   Date _____

B **Draw lines to match these.**

1. It is brown and black.

2. Where the dogs got a bath

3. It is a time.

4. How Jill and Dan feel

5. Tags has one.

6. It is not the front.

7. It is a good time.

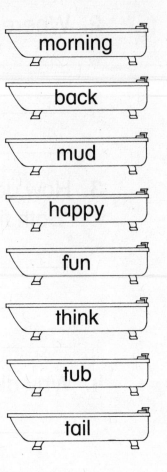

morning

back

mud

happy

fun

think

tub

tail

C **Read each sentence. Finish it.**
   Circle the right picture.

1. It is time for the dogs to eat. Wags went to _____.

   a.    b.   c.

2. Dan gets out of bed. He will get into the _____.

   a.    b.   c.

3. This is on your hand. It is your _____.

   a.    b.    c.

68

Selection 18
Core Skills Reading Comprehension, Grade 1

Name _____ Date _____

D **Who? What? Circle the right words.**

1. Jill saw the <u>mud</u>.

   Jill did not like | them
   it | .

2. Dan ran to the <u>dogs</u>.

   He went to | they
   them | .

3. The <u>dogs</u> jump in a puddle.

   | They
   It | are happy and wet!

4. I see the <u>bathtub</u>.

   It has water in | them
   it | .

5. <u>Jill</u> is not home.

   | He
   She | is not here.

E **Can you tell about selection 18? Some things are not in the right place. Put a 1, 2, and 3 in the boxes. One is done for you.**

| 1 | The dogs went into the tub.

| | The dogs ran out to play.

| | Jill and Dan were happy.

69

© Houghton Mifflin Harcourt Publishing Company

Selection 18
Core Skills Reading Comprehension, Grade 1

Selection 19

One day Mother Duck walked.
She walked on the grass.

She said, "Let's swim in the water.
You will do something new.
Do what I do.
It will be fun."

The ducks have food.
They got it in the pond.
The little ducks did something new.

A **Which one is right? Put a ✔ by it. One is done for you.**

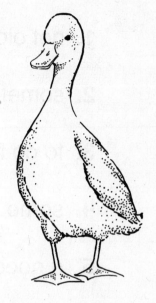

1. When did Mother Duck go for a walk?

   ___✔___ **a.** day

   _____ **b.** night

   _____ **c.** at the pond

2. Where did Mother take the baby ducks?

   _____ **a.** to the farm

   _____ **b.** to the water

   _____ **c.** to school

3. What new thing did the baby ducks do?

   _____ **a.** get food

   _____ **b.** go to sleep

   _____ **c.** play a game

4. How do baby ducks learn?

   _____ **a.** by reading a book

   _____ **b.** by eating fish

   _____ **c.** by looking at big ducks

5. What is the best name for this selection?

   _____ **a.** Baby Ducks Can Fly

   _____ **b.** Baby Ducks Run Away

   _____ **c.** Baby Ducks Do Something New

Name _____ Date _____

B **Draw lines to match the words.**
   One is done for you.

1. not old

2. something to eat

3. to go fast in the water

4. some water

5. a good time

6. something feet can do

food

fun

pond

new

do

walk

swim

C **Each picture goes with a sentence.**
   Draw lines to match them.

1. Flowers are in the pond.

2. A duck is flying.

3. Ducks swim.

4. The ducks walk
    with Mother.

5. A duck is eating.

a.

b.

c.

d.

72

Name _____ Date _____

D Read these selections. Answer the questions.

ONE

Ducks like to swim.

They swim in a pond.

They walk.

They eat food.

TWO

Mother Duck says, "Let's swim."

Baby Duck says, "That will be fun."

Mother and Baby Duck swim.

Baby Duck says, "I like to swim!"

1. The ducks talk in selection _____.

2. Selection _____ tells about real ducks.

E Can you tell about selection 19? Some things are not in the right place. Put a 1, 2, and 3 in the boxes. One is done for you.

☐ The ducks went into the water.

☐ They got food.

[1] The ducks walked on the grass.

73

Selection 20

One morning the robins were working.
They were making a nest.
The nest was in an old oak tree.
The father robin found some grass for the nest.
The mother got mud for the nest.
The nest was made of mud and grass.
Soon the mother will lay eggs in the nest.
The eggs will be blue.
What will come out of the robin's eggs?

A **Which one is right? Put a ✔ by it.**

1. When were the robins working?

_____ **a.** at night

_____ **b.** at noon

_____ **c.** in the morning

2. What were both the robins making?

_____ **a.** a school

_____ **b.** a home

_____ **c.** an oak tree

74

Name _____ Date _____

3. Where was the nest?

_____ **a.** in an apple tree

_____ **b.** in the brown sand

_____ **c.** in an oak tree

4. What was used to make the nest?

_____ **a.** grass and mud

_____ **b.** sand and mud

_____ **c.** grass and sand

5. What will the mother robin do?

_____ **a.** dig a hole

_____ **b.** lay eggs in the nest

_____ **c.** play and run

6. What color is a robin's egg?

_____ **a.** white   _____ **b.** brown   _____ **c.** blue

7. What will come out of the robin's eggs?

_____ **a.** baby chickens

_____ **b.** baby birds

_____ **c.** baby turtles

8. What is the best name for the selection?

_____ **a.** A Nest in the Sand

_____ **b.** A Nest in a Tree

_____ **c.** A Nest in the Grass

Name _____ Date _____

B **Draw lines to match these. One is done for you.**

1. green plants   robin

2. time of the day   morning

3. kind of bird   mother

4. what some women are called   grass

5. a tree   oak

6. color of a robin's egg   father

7. what some men are called   nest

8. home for birds   blue

                         make

C **Each picture goes with a sentence. Draw lines to match them.**

1. The robin finds some grass.   a.

2. Three eggs are in the nest.   b.

3. The robins make a nest.

4. The oak tree is big.   c.

5. Two eggs are in the nest.   d.

Selection 20
Core Skills Reading Comprehension, Grade 1

Name _____ Date _____

D **Who? What? Circle the right words.**

1. The <u>eggs</u> are blue.

   What will come out of | them
it | ?

2. <u>Father robin and mother robin</u> made a nest.

   | They
She | got grass for the nest.

3. Mother robin saw a <u>man</u>.

   Mother robin went away from | them
him | .

4. The birds live in the <u>tree</u>.

   They have a nest in | it
them | .

5. <u>Mother robin</u> will lay eggs soon.

   | Our
Her | eggs will be blue.

E **Do you know about the selection? Circle <u>yes</u> or <u>no</u>.**

1. Is the nest for the robin eggs?   yes   no

2. Do robins eat eggs?   yes   no

3. Are baby robins in the eggs?   yes   no

© Houghton Mifflin Harcourt Publishing Company

Selection 20
Core Skills Reading Comprehension, Grade 1

Selection 21

Part One

One afternoon, Mom said, "Ann and Andy, will you get me some food?"

Andy and I went to the store. We walked a long way down Duck Street. Then we went around a corner. We walked by the park. Then we got to the store.

Andy and I found eggs, bread, fish, and milk. A woman put the food into a bag for us. We gave the woman some money. Then Andy and I walked home.

Part Two

Andy and Ann gave me the bag of food. I looked inside. I said, "You forgot the lettuce."

"Sorry, Mom!" said Andy and Ann.

Andy and Ann had to go all the way back to the store. Then they walked home again.

A **Which one is right? Put a ✔ by it.**

  1. Who went to the store?

    _____ **a.** two children

    _____ **b.** Mom

    _____ **c.** two boys

2. Who tells part one?

_____ **a.** Mom

_____ **b.** Ann

_____ **c.** woman

3. What did Ann and Andy give the woman?

_____ **a.** food

_____ **b.** lettuce

_____ **c.** money

4. Who tells part two?

_____ **a.** Ann

_____ **b.** Andy

_____ **c.** Mom

5. Why did Ann and Andy go back to the store?

_____ **a.** to get money

_____ **b.** to get lettuce

_____ **c.** to see Mom there

6. What do we know about the store?

_____ **a.** It is a long way from home.

_____ **b.** It is next to Ann and Andy's house.

_____ **c.** It is on Old Street.

7. What is the best name for this selection?

_____ **a.** The Lost Lettuce

_____ **b.** Fun at the Store

_____ **c.** Two Long Walks

Name _____ Date _____

B **Draw lines to match these. One is done for you.**

1. a place to play

2. did not think about

3. a green food

4. a white drink

5. We pay with it.

6. boys and girls

7. a time of day

8. where two streets come together

lettuce

milk

park

forgot

corner

duck

afternoon

children

money

C **Pick out the right word from the bag.**
Write the word. One is done for you.

walk   black   milk
day   house   girl

1. lettuce, bread, eggs, ___milk___

2. school, store, home, _____

3. run, skip, jump, _____

4. Mom, woman, sister, _____

5. green, blue, brown, _____

80

D **Circle who tells each selection below.**

1. I went to the park with Ann.
   Ann said to me, "Andy, let's play!"
   Ann and I played together.

   Andy   Ann   Mom

2. Andy and Ann went to the store.
   They said, "Mom, can you make a cake?"
   I made them a big cake.

   Mom   Andy   Woman

3. Andy and I went to the park.
   Andy said, "Ann, let's feed the ducks!"

   Andy   duck   Ann

E **Can you tell about selection 21? Some things are not in the right place. Put a 1, 2, and 3 in the boxes.**

☐ Ann and Andy forgot to get the lettuce.

☐ Mom wanted some food from the store.

☐ Ann and Andy had to go back to the store.

81

Name _____ Date _____

Skills Review: Selections 17–21

A **Read the question. Write the answer next to each one.**
How many paws do they have? Write the words.

zero   one   four

 1. _____

 5. _____

 2. _____

 6. _____

 3. _____

 7. _____

 4. _____

 8. _____

B **Who? What? Circle the right words.**

1. <u>Dad</u> got some eggs at the store.

   | He |
   | She | took the eggs home.

2. <u>Mom</u> forgot to take the <u>bags</u>.

   She had to go home to get | it |
   | them | .

3. <u>Ann and Andy</u> ran around the corner.

   | They |
   | She | ran fast.

82

Name _____ Date _____

C **Draw lines to match these.**

1. a kind of bag

2. something to eat

3. time after morning

4. one more time

5. place to play

6. time for bed

7. not the back

pouch

afternoon

food

night

front

milk

park

again

D **Read each sentence. Finish it. Circle the right picture.**

1. The mother robin will lay a blue _____ in the nest.

a.    b.    c.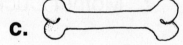

2. The kangaroo has a big _____.

a.    b.    c.

3. The little ducks eat _____.

a.    b.    c.

83

E **Circle the right word.**

1. We saw the kangaroo | hot / hop | in the tall grass.

2. Robins make a nest of | grass / green | and | mad / mud | .

3. Wags and Tags had a bath in a | top / tub | .

4. Ann and Andy | forgot / four | the lettuce.

5. They had to go | black / back | to the store.

6. Mother gave them | money / many | to get food.

7. Mother Duck walked on the | goats / grass | .

F **Can you tell about selection 21? Some things are not in the right place. Put a 1, 2, and 3 in the boxes.**

☐ A woman put the food into a bag.

☐ Mom asked Ann and Andy to get some food.

☐ Ann and Andy walked to the store.

Name _____ Date _____

G **Each picture goes with a sentence. Draw lines to match them.**

1.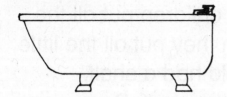

2.

3.

4.

5.

a. The baby gets big in the pouch.

b. People can get a bath in this tub.

c. Tags lives in this doghouse.

d. The robins look for food.

e. The children got them at the store.

f. The robins made a nest of grass and mud.

85

Selection 22

Mom and Dad wanted the children to take care of their toys. Every night the children put all the big toys in their rooms. Then they put all the little toys on a toy shelf. Each child had a shelf.

Bob was ten. He had the top shelf. Bev was eight. She had the middle shelf. Bill was seven. He had the bottom shelf.

On Sunday evening, Dad and Mom found lots of toys on the rug. They went to look at the toy shelf. They saw no toys on the middle shelf.

Mom said, "Now I know who did not put the toys away."

Can you guess who forgot to put away toys?

A **Which one is right? Put a ✔ by it.**

1. What was the selection about?

    _____ **a.** getting a new rug

    _____ **b.** getting a toy shelf

    _____ **c.** a child who forgot to do something

2. What did Mom and Dad want the children to do?

_____ **a.** go to the store

_____ **b.** put away the toys

_____ **c.** make a new shelf

3. Where did the children put their big toys?

_____ **a.** on a shelf

_____ **b.** under a bed

_____ **c.** in their rooms

4. When did Dad and Mom find toys on the rug?

_____ **a.** Tuesday evening

_____ **b.** Sunday evening

_____ **c.** Sunday afternoon

5. Who forgot to put the toys away?

_____ **a.** Bev _____ **b.** Bill _____ **c.** Bob

6. How did Mom know who did not put away toys?

_____ **a.** She saw toys on every shelf.

_____ **b.** She saw no toys on one shelf.

_____ **c.** She asked the children.

7. What is the lesson of this selection?

_____ **a.** Hide your toys.

_____ **b.** Put away your toys.

_____ **c.** Play with your toys.

Name _____ Date _____

B Draw lines to match these.

1. six and one

2. part that is under

3. day of the week

4. late in the day

5. seven and one

6. place to put things on

7. all of them

8. things to play with

9. not the top or the bottom

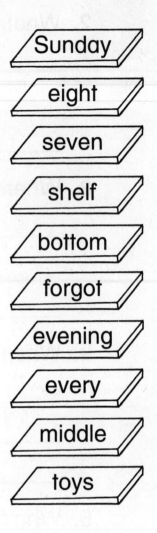

Sunday

eight

seven

shelf

bottom

forgot

evening

every

middle

toys

C Put some things on the big shelf.

1. Put a blue **X** on
   the middle shelf.

2. Put a brown ✔ on
   the bottom shelf.

3. Put a blue egg on
   the middle shelf.

4. Put a black box on
   the top shelf.

5. Put a red ▲ on
   every shelf.

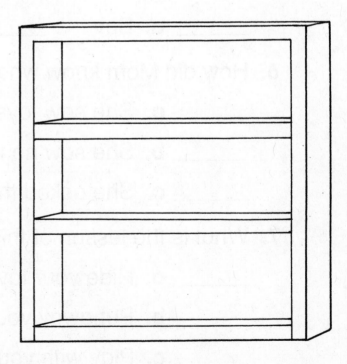

Name _____ Date _____

D **Circle one word that fits both sentences.**

too   top

1. A bird sat on _____ of the tree.

2. Bill played with his toy _____.

_____

play   day

3. Mom and Dad went to see a _____.

4. Children like to run and _____.

_____

can   care

5. The children must take _____ of the toys.

6. Bob did not _____ when Bev took his toy.

E **Look back at selection 22. Put the right child's name on each line.**

1. _____ was seven years old.

2. _____ was eight.

Bev

3. _____ was ten years old.

4. _____ had the top toy shelf.

Bill

5. _____ had the middle shelf.

6. _____ forgot to put away the toys.

Bob

Selection 22
Core Skills Reading Comprehension, Grade 1

Selection 23

Ducks like to be in water. They can swim fast. They play games in the water. They find food there, too. Ducks eat little bugs and fish. They pull plants out of the water to eat.

Ducks have big orange feet. The feet are good for pushing the water. Their feet make ducks good swimmers. Ducks' feet are not so good for walking and running. Their feet are not good for climbing.

Sometimes ducks must come out of the water. They cannot walk as well as they can swim. Ducks must take care on land. If ducks are not careful on land, a fox may catch them.

Why do you think a fox likes to catch a duck?

A **Which one is right? Put a ✔ by it.**

1. Why do foxes like to catch ducks?

_____ **a.** to make friends

_____ **b.** to play games

_____ **c.** for food

2. What do ducks like to eat?

_____ **a.** birds

_____ **b.** foxes

_____ **c.** bugs and plants

3. What can ducks use their feet to do?

_____ **a.** climb trees

_____ **b.** push water

_____ **c.** talk fast

4. Why don't foxes catch ducks in the water?

_____ **a.** Foxes don't swim well.

_____ **b.** Water is too cold.

_____ **c.** Ducks catch foxes.

5. Which animal is most like a duck?

_____ **a.** robin   _____ **b.** bee   _____ **c.** fox

6. What will you never see a duck do?

_____ **a.** climb a big tree

_____ **b.** eat in the water

_____ **c.** swim very fast

7. What is the best name for this selection?

_____ **a.** How Ducks Climb

_____ **b.** How Ducks Catch Bugs

_____ **c.** Why Ducks Like Water

Name _____ Date _____

B **What do you know about ducks? Circle the right answers.**

1. Which is the duck's foot?

   a.   **b.**   **c.**   **d.**

2. Do ducks eat candy?   yes   no

3. Do ducks have four feet?   yes   no

4. Do ducks eat water plants?   yes   no

5. Can ducks read books?   yes   no

6. Do ducks like ponds?   yes   no

7. Do ducks swim on land?   yes   no

8. Do ducks catch bugs?   yes   no

9. Can a fox catch a duck on land?   yes   no

C **Can you guess the riddles? Circle the right word.**

1. I am little.   2. I am an animal.
   I have many feet.   I have four feet.
   Ducks eat me.   Ducks must watch
   Children do not eat me.   out for me.
   What am I?   What am I?

   bag   bug   bird   bug   fox   bird

92

Name _____ Date _____

D Draw lines to match the opposites. One is done for you.

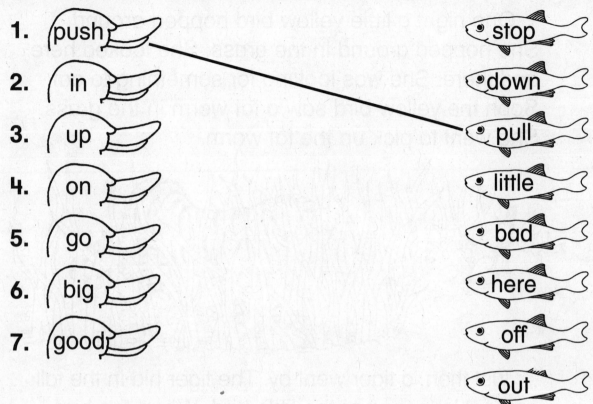

1. push
2. in
3. up
4. on
5. go
6. big
7. good

stop
down
pull
little
bad
here
off
out

E Look at a book's Table of Contents page. You can see the number of the page where each story starts. Can you answer these?

1. Circle the page number on which you can find **Fish's Home**.

2. What story starts on page 8?
   _____
   -
   _____

3. Is there a story about a turtle in this book?
   _____
   -
   _____

Stories	
Bug's Toy	2
Fish's Home	4
Lost Duck	5
Baby Monkey	7
Rabbit's House	8

Selection 23
Core Skills Reading Comprehension, Grade 1

Selection 24

One night a little yellow bird hopped around. She hopped around in the grass. She looked here and there. She was looking for something to eat. Soon the yellow bird saw a fat worm in the grass. She went to pick up the fat worm.

Just then, a tiger went by. The tiger hid in the tall grass. He looked at the little bird. When the bird pulled at the worm, the tiger jumped! He jumped at the yellow bird! He wanted to eat the bird.

But birds are quick. The little yellow bird got away! She flew far away. The tiger was left with the fat worm.

And tigers do not like to eat worms!

A Which one is right? Put a ✔ by it.

1. What is this selection about?

_____ **a.** a tiger eating

_____ **b.** a fast bird

_____ **c.** what worms eat

2. What was the bird doing?

_____ **a.** looking for food

_____ **b.** sitting in a tree

_____ **c.** looking for a tiger

3. What was the tiger doing?

_____ **a.** eating worms

_____ **b.** flying away

_____ **c.** looking for food

4. Where was the bird?

_____ **a.** in a tree

_____ **b.** in a nest

_____ **c.** in the grass

5. When was the bird looking for food?

_____ **a.** in the morning

_____ **b.** in the afternoon

_____ **c.** at night

6. Who got some food?

_____ **a.** no one

_____ **b.** the tiger

_____ **c.** the bird

7. What color was the bird?

_____ **a.** brown   _____ **b.** yellow   _____ **c.** blue

95

8. What do you think the worm did?

    _____ **a.** ate the bird

    _____ **b.** got away

    _____ **c.** looked for a tiger

9. A **quick** tiger is a _____ tiger.

    _____ **a.** pretty   _____ **b.** little   _____ **c.** fast

10. What is the best name for this selection?

    _____ **a.** The Tiger's Dinner

    _____ **b.** How Worms Get Birds

    _____ **c.** The Bird That Got Away

B **Read the words on the worms. Then read what to do. Can you mark the right words?**

tiger   worm   hopped   tall

hunt   left   green   quick

1. Make a ✔ on the word that means **jumped**.

2. Circle the name of the animal with four feet.

3. Put a box around the color of grass.

4. Put an **X** on the word that means **went away**.

5. Circle the word that means **big**.

6. Put a △ on the word that means **to look for**.

7. Put a line under the word that means **fast**.

C Put a ✔ by each one that is right about selection 24.

_____ **1.** The tiger found some grass to eat.

_____ **2.** The worm wanted to eat a fat tiger.

_____ **3.** Tigers like to eat worms.

_____ **4.** The bird pulled at the worm.

_____ **5.** Birds like to eat worms.

_____ **6.** The bird got away fast.

_____ **7.** The bird picked up the tiger.

_____ **8.** The worm was fat.

_____ **9.** The tiger hid in the tall grass.

D What are Betty Bird and Will Worm doing? Put a ✔ by each sentence that tells what they are doing.

1. _____ **a.** Betty hunts for food.

_____ **b.** Betty hops into the water.

_____ **c.** Betty plays with a tiger.

2. _____ **a.** Will hid in a box.

_____ **b.** Will hid in the grass.

_____ **c.** Will hid in an apple.

3. _____ **a.** Betty Bird pulls on a worm.

_____ **b.** Will Worm pulls on a bird.

_____ **c.** The bird and worm play.

97

Name _____ Date _____

Selection 25

RACE DAY
by Kim Black

MONDAY   Today was race day. There were five races. The races were on the school playground.

Mr. Pack started the races. He told the children to stand side-by-side.

"Get ready. One! Two! Three! Go!" called Mr. Pack.

Ten children ran in the last race. Away went the children. They raced faster and faster. Other children watched.

"Hurry! Hurry! Run faster!" the other children called out.

Lupe fell down. Then he could not run again. Pam's shoe came off. She had to stop, too!

Mr. Pack called, "May wins the race!"

Jeff came in second, with Rita after him. Ted was last in the race. It was a good race day!

A **How did they do in the last race? Look at the report again. Write the names on the lines.**

first   next

1. _____   3. _____

second   last

2. _____   4. _____

Selection 25

Core Skills Reading Comprehension, Grade 1

Name _____   Date _____

B **Which one is right? Put a ✔ by it.**

1. What is this report about?

    _____ **a.** Mr. Pack's playground

    _____ **b.** a boat race

    _____ **c.** race day

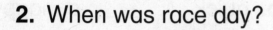

2. When was race day?

    _____ **a.** Monday

    _____ **b.** Tuesday

    _____ **c.** Sunday

3. Who watched the race?

    _____ **a.** children   _____ **b.** fathers   _____ **c.** mothers

4. Why did Pam stop running?

    _____ **a.** She fell.

    _____ **b.** She saw her friend.

    _____ **c.** Her shoe came off.

5. Who stopped running before the last race was over?

    _____ **a.** two girls

    _____ **b.** a boy and a girl

    _____ **c.** two boys

6. How many children ran to the end of the last race?

    _____ **a.** ten   _____ **b.** nine   _____ **c.** eight

7. Who came in before Rita?

_____ **a.** Jeff   _____ **b.** Ted   _____ **c.** Bob

8. Who won the last race?

_____ **a.** Rita   _____ **b.** Jeff   _____ **c.** May

9. If you **hurry**, you are _____.

_____ **a.** sad   _____ **b.** quick   _____ **c.** happy

C **Draw lines to match these.**

1. to go very fast

2. It is on a foot.

3. a place to learn

4. after the first

5. looked at

6. made it begin

7. name of a day

8. set to go

9. at the end

10. a place to play

11. a game to see who can go fast

second

hurry

school

side

Monday

shoe

started

race

watched

last

playground

ready

Name _____ Date _____

D **Read each action word. When you put er on the action word, you name a person who does the action.**

1. help — helper   4. play — player
2. start — starter   5. win — winner
3. run — runner   6. jump — jumper

Circle the right word for each sentence.

1. Mr. Pack will _____ the races.

   start   starter

2. May was the _____ of the last race.

   win   winner

3. There were ten _____ in the race.

   run   runners

4. Lupe fell and could not _____ again.

   run   runner

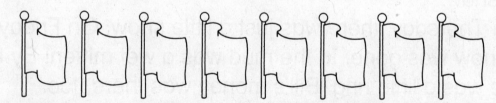

E **Fun Time! Can you do this?**

1. How many flags do you see? _____
2. Color the first one blue.
3. Color the last one yellow.
4. Color the second one green.
5. Circle the next to the last one.
6. Color the next to the last one brown.
7. Color four others red.

101

Name _____ Date _____

Selection 26

It snowed all day on Monday. On Tuesday, Pat and Bill played in the white snow. They jumped and fell in it.

Bill lost one mitten and some money. Pat lost her ring in the deep, deep snow.

"I want my ring," said Pat. "Please help me find it, Mom!" Mom said, "No, Pat. The snow is too deep."

"Where is my money?" asked Bill. "No one will help me find it."

Then Dad said, "Soon something big and yellow will help you find the lost things."

On Wednesday, the sun was in the sky. There was less snow.

On Thursday, there was just a little snow. On Friday, the snow was gone. In the mud was a wet mitten! By the fence was a little ring. Bill's money was there, too.

Who was the children's helper?

A **Which one is right? Put a ✔ by it.**

1. When did the snow start to fall?

_____ **a.** Monday

_____ **b.** Wednesday

_____ **c.** Thursday

2. How do you think Bill's money got lost?

_____ **a.** Pat hid it in the snow.

_____ **b.** When Bill fell, the money dropped out.

_____ **c.** Someone took it out of his mitten.

3. Why didn't Pat find her ring?

_____ **a.** The trees hid it.

_____ **b.** Pat left it in her room.

_____ **c.** The snow was too deep.

4. Where was the ring?

_____ **a.** under the tree

_____ **b.** by the fence

_____ **c.** under the flowers

5. What came first in the selection?

_____ **a.** A mitten was found.

_____ **b.** Pat asked Mom for help.

_____ **c.** They played in the snow.

6. Who was the children's helper?

_____ **a.** a truck   _____ **b.** the moon   _____ **c.** the sun

7. What is the best name for this selection?

_____ **a.** Fun in the Mud

_____ **b.** The Sun and the Snow

_____ **c.** The Lost Fence

Name _____ Date _____

B **Draw lines to match these.**

1. not as much

2. something for hands

3. cannot be found

4. It falls from the sky.

5. the color of snow

6. day after Wednesday

7. a penny

Thursday

white

money

mittens

Tuesday

lost

snow

less

C **Which one is right? Put a ✔ by it.**

1. Three of us came into the room. I came in first.
   Bill came in last. Pat was _____.

   _____ **a.** the last one

   _____ **b.** the first one

   _____ **c.** the middle one

2. Pat and Bill wanted to go to the zoo on Monday.
   Mom and Dad had to work on Monday. Dad said
   they would all go to the zoo the next day. When
   will they go to the zoo?

   _____ **a.** on Monday

   _____ **b.** on Tuesday

   _____ **c.** on Sunday

104

Name _____ Date _____

D **Write the days in order.**

Friday   Wednesday   Tuesday   Monday   Thursday

1. __Sunday__

2. _____

3. _____

4. _____

5. _____

6. _____

7. __Saturday__

E **Read each selection. Circle the words that tell about it.**

1. The sun is hot. It helps the trees get big. It melts the snow. This selection is about the _____.

   a. trees   **b.** sun   **c.** flowers

2. On Monday, there was a lot of snow. The sun came out on Tuesday. On Wednesday, there was less snow. On Thursday, the snow was gone.
   This selection is about _____.

   a. how the snow hid the cars
   b. how deep the snow was
   c. how the snow melted

3. Bill's cat was by the fence. The snow fell. The cat ran into the house. Bill had to dry the cat's feet.
   This selection is about _____.

   a. wet mittens   **b.** wet feet   **c.** wet money

Skills Review: Selections 22–26

A **Read this selection.**

All the children are going to a show.
Bev is going to the show on Monday.
Lupe is going the day before Bev.
Jeff is going the day after Bev.
Rita is going the day before Sunday.
Pat is going the day after Tuesday.

When are they going to the show? Draw lines to match each child to the right day.

1.  Pat

          a. Sunday

          b. Monday

2.  Rita

          c. Tuesday

3.  Bev

          d. Wednesday

4.  Lupe

          e. Thursday

          f. Friday

5.  Jeff

          g. Saturday

Skills Review: Selections 22–26
Core Skills Reading Comprehension, Grade 1

Name _____   Date _____

B **Each shelf must have three words. Put the words below on the right shelves.**

Colors	Numbers	Animals

1. tiger   5. seven   8. green
2. yellow   6. white   9. nine
3. eight   7. duck   10. again
4. worm

C **Draw lines to match these.**

1. not as much

2. to look for

3. after the first

4. went away

5. late in the day

6. at the end

7. fast

8. all of them

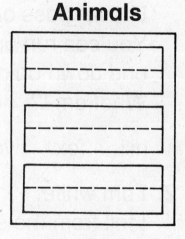

snow

left

less

evening

hunt

second

every

quick

last

Skills Review: Selections 22–26
Core Skills Reading Comprehension, Grade 1

Name _____ Date _____

D **Can you guess the riddles? Circle the right word.**

1. I go up, up, up.
   I have grass on me.
   You can run up
   and down on me.
   What am I?

   hill   fox   water

2. I am white.
   I fall from the sky.
   I fall on cold days.
   Children play with me.
   What am I?

   sun   rain   snow

3. I am wet.
   Fish live in me.
   Children swim in me.
   Ducks sit on me.
   What am I?

   water   hill   box

4. I am a swimmer.
   I like the water.
   I have no feet.
   You like to catch me.
   What am I?

   fox   fish   duck

5. I am little.
   Birds try to get me.
   I have no feet.
   I stay in the grass.
   What am I?

   worm   fox   cat

6. I can run fast.
   I run after birds.
   I have four legs.
   I do not eat worms.
   What am I?

   bug   duck   tiger

108

Name _____ Date _____

E **Can you do this?**

1. Put an **X** on the middle book.
2. Color the top book green.
3. Color the bottom book orange.

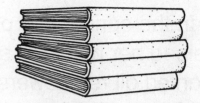

4. Make a hole in the bottom.
5. Color the hole brown.
6. Color the shoe yellow.

F **Circle the _one_ word that fits both sentences.**

        last   left

1. Turn _____ at the corner.

2. The bird _____ in a hurry.

        last   left

3. I was _____ in line.

4. The race will _____ a long time.

G **Can you do this?**

1. Put an **X** on the page
   where **Jeff's Ring** starts.

2. Put a line under the story
   found on page 8.

3. Circle the page number on
   which you can find **A Lost Puppy**.

Stories

Jeff's Ring 3
A Lost Puppy 6
The Ice Melts 8

109

Selection 27

In the spring, Fay planted seeds in a window box. Pete helped her plant the seeds. They liked the color red. They planted all red flowers.

Little green plants came up first. Then red flowers came out of the green plants. The window box looked very pretty.

Two birds came to the window box. The birds had some seeds in their beaks. One bird dropped a seed. The seed fell into the window box. Fay and Pete did not see the birds.

One day, the children looked at their pretty red flowers. They saw a big purple flower with all the red flowers! What a surprise!

"How did the purple flower get there?" asked Pete.

"I do not know," said Fay. "We planted all red flowers."

They never found out how the purple flower got there. Do you know?

Name _____ Date _____

A **Which one is right? Put a ✔ by it.**

1. When did Fay plant seeds in the window box?

   _____ **a.** fall   _____ **b.** winter   _____ **c.** spring

2. What is this selection about?

   _____ **a.** a big red flower

   _____ **b.** what birds eat

   _____ **c.** a purple surprise

3. What came out of the seeds first?

   _____ **a.** red flowers

   _____ **b.** green plants

   _____ **c.** brown birds

4. Why did the birds have seeds?

   _____ **a.** to plant them

   _____ **b.** to eat them

   _____ **c.** for gifts to the children

5. How did the purple flower get into the box?

   _____ **a.** Pete planted it there.

   _____ **b.** Fay put it there as a surprise.

   _____ **c.** A bird dropped a seed.

6. What is the best name for this selection?

   _____ **a.** A Big Surprise

   _____ **b.** Pretty Colors

   _____ **c.** A Nest in the Window Box

Name _____ Date _____

B **Draw lines to match these.**

1. time of year

2. We look out of it.

3. at no time

4. saw where it was

5. a color

6. put seeds in the ground

7. something we did not know about

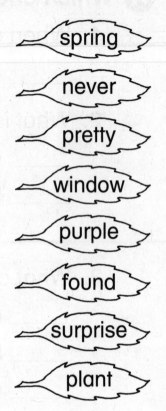

spring

never

pretty

window

purple

found

surprise

plant

C **Circle the right word.**

1. Little plants came [us / up] .

2. Two birds [can / came] to the window.

3. I saw a seed [drop / chop] into the box.

4. How did the seed get [there / they] ?

5. They [every / never] did find out.

D **Read these sentences.**

1. How did the purple flower get here**?**
2. I did not plant purple flowers**.**

The first sentence **asks** something. Use a **?** at the end.
The second sentence **tells** something. Use a **.** at the end.

Put a ? or a . at the end of each sentence.

1. Fay planted some seeds

2. Did Pete help plant seeds

3. Will little green plants come up first

4. Then flowers came out of the plants

5. A seed fell into the window box

6. Did a bird drop the seed

E **Find the sentence that means the same as the first one.**
Put a ✔ by it.

1. They planted all red flowers.

    _____ Every flower they planted was red.

    _____ They planted one red flower.

2. Little green plants came up first.

    _____ Little green plants came up after the flowers.

    _____ Little green plants came up before the flowers.

3. The purple flower was a surprise.

    _____ They planted the purple flower.

    _____ They did not know the purple flower was there.

Selection 28

Mr. and Mrs. Hill had three children. Jay was ten years old. Kay was eight. Ray was six years old.

One afternoon, Ray came home from school. He had lost some of his things. He had lost his new book bag! He had lost his lunchbox! And he had even lost all the buttons from his coat!

  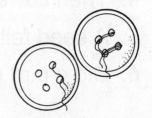

Mrs. Hill said, "Let's help Ray find his things." The family hunted and looked. Jay found two buttons around the corner. Kay found one button in the doghouse. Mrs. Hill found one button by the flowers. Mr. Hill saw the book bag under a tree. But they did not find the lunchbox.

The next day, Ray went to school again. There was his lunchbox by a window. Ray had left it there.

A Which one is right? Put a ✔ by it.

1. How old was Ray?

_____ **a.** seven _____ **b.** four _____ **c.** six

Name _____ Date _____

2. What is this selection about?

_____ **a.** a lost girl

_____ **b.** two boys who lost things

_____ **c.** how the family helped Ray

3. How many buttons were on Ray's coat?

_____ **a.** four   _____ **b.** three   _____ **c.** two

4. Who found the lunchbox?

_____ **a.** Kay   _____ **b.** Ray   _____ **c.** Jay

5. Who found two buttons?

_____ **a.** Kay   _____ **b.** Ray   _____ **c.** Jay

6. Who found the book bag?

_____ **a.** Mrs. Hill

_____ **b.** Mr. Hill

_____ **c.** Kay Hill

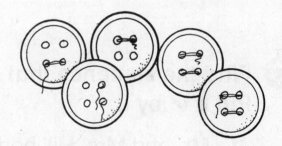

7. How did the book bag get under the tree?

_____ **a.** Kay put it there.

_____ **b.** Ray put it there and forgot it.

_____ **c.** The book bag walked there.

8. What must Ray learn to do?

_____ **a.** stay at home

_____ **b.** get a new coat

_____ **c.** take care of his things

Name _____ Date _____

B **Where was each thing found? Draw lines to match them.**

PLACES

THINGS

1. around the corner

a.

2. under a tree

b.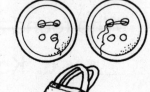

3. by the flowers

c.

4. in a doghouse

d.

5. at school

e.

C **Find the sentence that means the same as the first one. Put a ✔ by it.**

1. Mr. and Mrs. Hill had three children.

_____ They had three girls and one boy.

_____ They had one girl and two boys.

2. Ray left the school at noon.

_____ He went into the school at noon.

_____ He came out of the school at noon.

3. They lost the book again.

_____ They lost the book one more time.

_____ They never lost the book.

116

Core Skills Reading Comprehension, Grade 1

D **Draw lines to match these.**

1. two and one

2. a man

3. did not find

4. let us

5. noon meal

6. It is on a coat.

let's

Mr.

button

Mrs.

lost

three

lunch

E **Put the words that tell <u>where</u> in the <u>WHERE?</u> box. Put the words that tell <u>when</u> in the <u>WHEN?</u> box. Draw lines to the right box. The first one is done for you.**

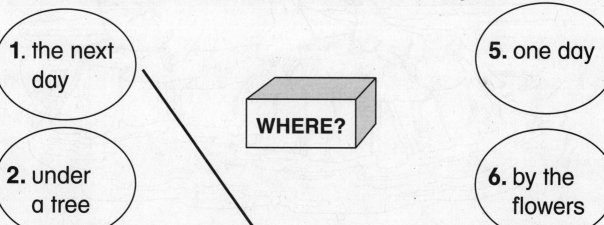

1. the next day

2. under a tree

3. on the window

4. at night

5. one day

6. by the flowers

7. in the house

8. after lunch

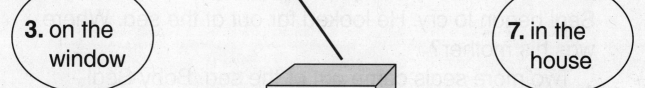

WHERE?

WHEN?

117

Selection 29

Baby Seal was asleep on a big rock. Mother Seal was gone. She went to look for food in the water.

Baby Seal got up and looked around. He saw many big mother seals. But he did not see his mother.

A mother seal came up out of the water. Baby Seal barked, "Mother!" He went over to her. The mother seal looked at him.

"You are not my little pup!" she barked. Then Baby Seal began to cry. He looked far out at the sea. Where was his mother?

Two more seals came out of the sea. Baby Seal barked a happy seal bark. He could smell his mother. His mother could smell him.

Baby seals know their mothers. Mother seals know their babies. Now Baby Seal had found his mother.

A **Which one is right? Put a ✔ by it.**

1. This selection is about a seal

   _____ **a.** looking for its home.

   _____ **b.** looking for its mother.

   _____ **c.** looking for a friend.

2. What are baby seals called?

   _____ **a.** pups   _____ **b.** kids   _____ **c.** kittens

3. What noise do seals make?

   _____ **a.** mew   _____ **b.** bark   _____ **c.** moo

4. Which one came first?

   _____ **a.** Baby Seal found his mother.

   _____ **b.** A seal said, "You are not my little pup."

   _____ **c.** Baby Seal began to cry.

5. Why did Baby Seal cry?

   _____ **a.** He wanted to go to sleep.

   _____ **b.** He fell into the cold water.

   _____ **c.** He wanted to be with his mother.

6. How do mother seals know their babies?

   _____ **a.** by their smell

   _____ **b.** by their look

   _____ **c.** by their cry

Selection 29
Core Skills Reading Comprehension, Grade 1

B **Draw lines to match these.**

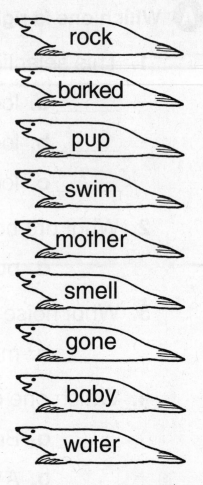

1. baby seal or dog

2. She takes care of her children.

3. something seals sit on

4. not here

5. a very little child

6. made a dog noise

7. move in the water

8. tell with your nose

rock

barked

pup

swim

mother

smell

gone

baby

water

C **Every sentence has a mark at the end that says "Stop!"**
A sentence that <u>asks</u> you something has a ? at the end.
A sentence that <u>tells</u> you something has a . at the end.
Put a ? or a . at the end of each sentence.

1. What did the seals find in the sea

2. Is the water cold

3. The seals barked

4. Is the rock too big to pick up

5. Seals can smell each other

6. Could they see any seals

7. Who began to cry

8. Did they eat many fish

120

Name _____ Date _____

a. Zoo Animals

b. Plants to Grow

c. Work We Do

D **Look at the three books. Which book would you use to find out about each thing? Write a letter in each box. The first one is done for you.**

b	**1.** flowers that grow fast
	2. how to put out fires
	3. animals that live in water
	4. tigers and monkeys
	5. little trees
	6. cleaning the streets
	7. building a house
	8. seeds of many kinds
	9. working on cars
	10. animals that can fly

Selection 30

One afternoon Roy and Rosa were at the pond. Rosa saw something on a water plant. She said, "Here is something funny. What can it be, Roy?"

The thing looked like jelly. It had little black spots in it.

The children put the thing into a big jar with water. They took it home. They watched it every day.

After six days, tadpoles came out of the eggs. They had long tails.

Soon back legs began to come out. The tails got shorter.

Then front legs began to come out. The tails got even shorter.

All four legs got big. The tails were gone!

Rosa said, "Now I know. I found frog eggs. Tadpoles came out of the eggs. Tadpoles are baby frogs!"

A Which one is right? Put a ✔ by it.

1. Who found something?

_____ **a.** a girl

_____ **b.** a boy

_____ **c.** a frog

2. Where did they see something funny?

_____ **a.** in the water

_____ **b.** in the sand

_____ **c.** on a shelf

3. What is a tadpole?

_____ **a.** a baby fish

_____ **b.** a little duck

_____ **c.** a baby frog

4. What looked like jelly?

_____ **a.** tadpoles   _____ **b.** frogs   _____ **c.** eggs

5. What came out first?

_____ **a.** front legs   _____ **b.** back legs   _____ **c.** boots

6. What happened to the tadpole?

_____ **a.** Its tail got very big.

_____ **b.** It became an egg.

_____ **c.** It became a frog.

7. What is the best name for this selection?

_____ **a.** What the Frog Found

_____ **b.** What Rosa Found

_____ **c.** A Bad Frog

123

B **Draw lines to match these.**

1. something to hold water

2. the opposite of **back**

3. something to walk on

4. something on the back of animals

5. not as long

6. something to eat on bread

tadpoles

front

jelly

legs

jar

tails

shorter

C **When? Where? Go for a walk with the children. Put a ✔ on the ones that tell <u>when</u>. Put an X on the ones that tell <u>where</u>.**

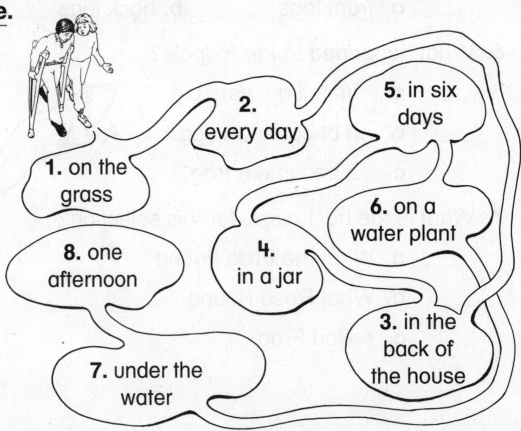

1. on the grass

2. every day

5. in six days

6. on a water plant

8. one afternoon

4. in a jar

3. in the back of the house

7. under the water

D **Fun time! Read the sentence. Finish it. Circle the right picture.**

1. Roy put the funny thing in a _____.

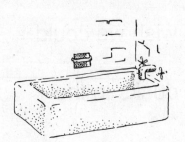

a.   b.   c.

2. They found eggs in the _____.

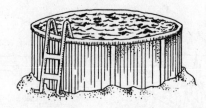

a.   b.   c.

3. A front door is found on a _____.

a.   b.   c.

4. Roy and Rosa found something that looks like _____.

a.   b.   c.

Selection 31

One afternoon, a mother fox was out looking for food. Her two little foxes were with her. They saw some ducks in the pond.

Fred Fox said, "I like to eat duck. I wish we could catch one."

Mother Fox said, "We can't catch ducks in the water. They can swim too fast."

The foxes hid in the tall grass. They watched the ducks playing in the pond. At last, eight ducks came out on the land.

Mother Fox said, "Now we can catch a duck. Ducks don't walk fast."

"I'll grab that first duck," said Fran Fox.

"I'll grab that last duck," said Fred Fox.

Mother Fox said, "Wait until they get near us. Ready? Go!" The foxes jumped out of the grass.

As quick as can be, the ducks got away. Did they run away? No! Did they swim away? No! The ducks flew away!

Mother Fox said, "I forgot that ducks have wings. Now we have nothing to eat!"

Name _____ Date _____

Ⓐ **Which one is right? Put a ✔ by it.**

1. Which one happened first?

_____ **a.** The foxes jumped at the ducks.

_____ **b.** The ducks came out of the water.

_____ **c.** The ducks got away.

2. Where did the ducks play?

_____ **a.** in the pond

_____ **b.** in the barn

_____ **c.** in the yard

3. Why did the foxes wait before jumping?

_____ **a.** They wanted to surprise the ducks.

_____ **b.** They wanted some help.

_____ **c.** They wanted Mother Fox to rest.

4. How did the ducks get away?

_____ **a.** by walking fast

_____ **b.** by jumping in the pond

_____ **c.** by flying away

5. What helps a duck fly?

_____ **a.** feet   _____ **b.** water   _____ **c.** wings

6. What is the best name for this selection?

_____ **a.** A Good Dinner for the Foxes

_____ **b.** No Dinner for the Foxes

_____ **c.** Fred Fox Gets a Duck

127

Name _____ Date _____

B **Draw lines to match these.**

1. not far

2. take away fast

3. not anything

4. water to swim in

5. animals

6. to want

7. up to the time of

8. They help birds fly.

9. ground

nothing

pond

near

last

grab

foxes

until

wish

land

wings

C **A sentence that <u>tells</u> something ends with a period. A sentence that <u>asks</u> something ends with a question mark. Put a . or a ? at the end of each sentence.**

1. Are you ready to catch a duck

2. The foxes hid in the grass

3. The ducks played in the pond

4. Can foxes catch ducks in the water

5. Did the ducks run away

6. The ducks did not swim away

7. Do ducks have wings

8. Why did the ducks fly away

9. How many ducks did the foxes grab

128

Name _____ Date _____

D **Find the sentence that means the same as the first one. Put a ✔ by it.**

1. They were by a pond.

_____ **a.** They were near a fence.

_____ **b.** They were near the water.

_____ **c.** They were near the tall grass.

2. Fran walked last.

_____ **a.** Fran was in the middle.

_____ **b.** Fran was in back.

_____ **c.** Fran was first.

E **Find the sentence that goes with each picture. Put the right letter under the picture.**

      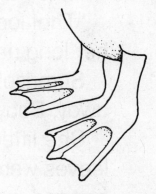

1. _____   2. _____   3. _____

a. A duck's feet can push the water.

b. Birds use them to fly.

c. This animal likes to eat ducks.

d. The ducks fly over the pond.

129

Name _____ Date _____

Selection 32

One afternoon Mom Giraffe went to the water hole. She went to get a drink. Baby Giraffe did not want to go with her mother.

Mom Giraffe said, "Stay here, Baby Pat, and do not go away."

Soon Pat wanted something good to eat. She forgot what her mom told her.

She walked into the tall grass. She saw a fat worm.

Pat wanted to eat the worm. But Pat was too tall. The worm crawled away.

Next Pat saw a little bird on a nest.

"That looks good to eat," said Pat as she bent her long neck to reach the tiny animal.

Surprise! Little birds have wings. The bird flew away. Baby Pat said, "Birds are too fast for me."

She lifted her long neck. Pretty green leaves were right by her mouth. Her mouth opened, and Pat ate the leaves.

Dad Giraffe came by. "Good for you!" he said. "You have found the best food for giraffes. You found it by yourself."

130

© Houghton Mifflin Harcourt Publishing Company

Selection 32

Core Skills Reading Comprehension, Grade 1

A **Which one is right? Put a ✔ by it.**

1. Which one happens first?

_____ **a.** The worm crawls away.

_____ **b.** The giraffe sees a worm.

_____ **c.** The giraffe eats some leaves.

2. Where did Mom Giraffe go?

_____ **a.** to the water hole

_____ **b.** to the big tree

_____ **c.** to see the bird in the nest

3. Why are leaves the best food for giraffes to eat?

_____ **a.** The leaves are pretty and are by the water hole.

_____ **b.** Long necks help giraffes reach leaves on tall trees.

_____ **c.** Giraffes can reach down to little animals under the grass.

4. What words tell about giraffes?

_____ **a.** long neck, long legs, wings

_____ **b.** short back legs, short tail, long fat neck

_____ **c.** long legs, long neck, spots on fur

5. What is the best name for this selection?

_____ **a.** Dad at the Water Hole

_____ **b.** A Giraffe Helps Herself

_____ **c.** Mom Giraffe Finds a Drink

Name _____ Date _____

B Draw lines to match these.

1. to get up to something

2. very little

3. where to put food

4. to take away fast

5. to move slowly along the ground

6. picked up

7. look at something for a long time

8. They help birds fly.

9. It holds up your head.

10. It is what we do with milk.

grab

drink

neck

crawl

bent

watch

reach

tiny

lifted

mouth

wings

C Do the animals eat plants or meat? If they eat other animals, they are meat eaters. Write <u>plants</u> next to the plant eaters. Write <u>meat</u> next to the meat eaters.

 1. _____

 2. _____

 3. _____

 4. _____

132

Selection 32
Core Skills Reading Comprehension, Grade 1

Name _____ Date _____

D Find the sentence that means the same as the first one. Put a ✔ by it.

1. Ray can reach the shelf.

_____ **a.** He can play with it.

_____ **b.** He can get to it.

_____ **c.** He cannot get to it.

2. Baby Giraffe walked in front of the others.

_____ **a.** She was in the middle.

_____ **b.** She was the first.

_____ **c.** She was in back.

3. They lifted a frog.

_____ **a.** They saw an animal.

_____ **b.** They picked up an animal.

_____ **c.** They put down an animal.

E Put a ✔ by the words that tell <u>where</u>. Put an X by the words that tell <u>when</u>.

1. _____ that evening

2. _____ into her pouch

3. _____ before dinner

4. _____ on the leaves

5. _____ on the grass

6. _____ after school

7. _____ all day

8. _____ under the nest

133

Selection 33: Paired

A desert is a hot place with very little water.
It can be hard to find food and water. It is hot
during the day. It is cool at night. Some desert
animals are camels, rabbits, snakes, and lizards.
Many animals sleep during the day. They look for
food at night.

Desert plants and animals have special parts.
The parts help them live in dry places. A cactus
has thick stems. It has waxy skin. The stems and
skin hold water. A camel has wide feet. Its feet
help it walk in the sand.

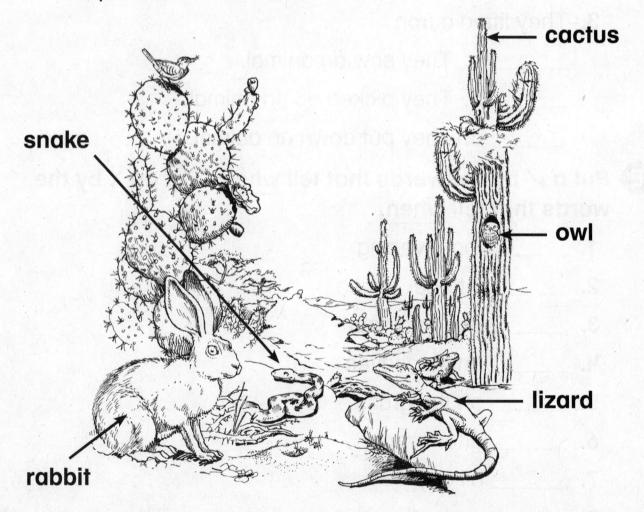

cactus

snake

owl

lizard

rabbit

Name _____ Date _____

A **Which one is right? Put a ✔ by it.**

1. What is a desert?

_____ **a.** a hot place

_____ **b.** a plant

_____ **c.** an animal

2. What can be hard to find in a desert?

_____ **a.** sand

_____ **b.** water

_____ **c.** animals

3. Why can camels walk in the desert?

_____ **a.** They have wide feet.

_____ **b.** They have a thick stem.

_____ **c.** They have two legs.

4. What parts help a cactus live in the desert?

_____ **a.** flowers

_____ **b.** wide feet

_____ **c.** waxy skin

5. What tells you where an owl lives?

_____ **a.** the selection

_____ **b.** the picture

_____ **c.** the selection and the picture

135

B **Circle the right word.**

1. What animal has wide feet?

   owl   camel   snake

2. What word means **not wet**?

   dry   hard   thick

3. What is a kind of plant?

   skin   rock   cactus

4. What is a hot, dry place?

   desert   lizard   stem

5. What word means **not much**?

   special   waxy   little

C **Find the sentence that goes with each picture. Put the right letter under the picture.**

   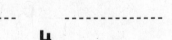

1. _____   2. _____   3. _____   4. _____

   a. The cactus has thick stems.

   b. The owl has big eyes.

   c. The snake is long.

   d. The rabbit hops.

Name _____ Date _____

D **Can you guess the riddles? Circle the right word.**

1. I am a plant.
   I have thick stems.
   I hold water in my stems
      and skin.
   I live in the desert.
   What am I?

2. I am an animal.
   I have wide feet.
   I can walk in sand.
   I live in the desert.
   What am I?

   camel cactus rock   lizard rabbit camel

E **Circle the right word.**

1. The camel walks in the | sand |
                            | snake | .

2. A cactus has waxy | stem |
                       | skin | .

3. Desert plants and animals have special | parts |
                                            | pets | .

4. Many desert animals look for food at | noon |
                                          | night | .

© Houghton Mifflin Harcourt Publishing Company

Selection 34: Paired

In the daytime, deserts can get very hot! Deserts can be made of sand, soil, or rocks. Deserts are dry. You may think that no animals could live in this hot, dry land. But many animals are found in deserts.

Some desert animals, like lizards, spend the hot daytime hours in the shade. They come out only to find food and water. They come out in the cool early morning and late afternoon.

Other desert animals come out to eat and drink only at night. Foxes and skunks sleep in their dens all day. Bats and many snakes also sleep all day and hunt all night.

Ⓐ Which one is right? Put a ✔ by it.

1. What words tell about a desert?

_____ **a.** cold, snow, ice

_____ **b.** cool, wet, rain

_____ **c.** hot, dry, rocks

2. What can you see in a desert?

_____ **a.** water

_____ **b.** sand

_____ **c.** grass

3. When do lizards find food?

_____ **a.** in the early morning

_____ **b.** at night

_____ **c.** at lunchtime

4. What is it like in the shade?

_____ **a.** hot

_____ **b.** cool

_____ **c.** wet

5. When are most desert animals awake?

_____ **a.** all day

_____ **b.** at night

_____ **c.** only in the late afternoon

6. When do snakes hunt?

_____ **a.** in the morning

_____ **b.** in the afternoon

_____ **c.** at night

7. What animal could you find in the desert?

_____ **a.** fish

_____ **b.** skunk

_____ **c.** cow

8. What is the best name for this selection?

_____ **a.** Hunting

_____ **b.** Lizards and Foxes

_____ **c.** Animals in the Desert

B **Draw lines to match these. One is done for you.**

1. early in the day   (afternoon)

2. They fly.   (shade)

3. when it is dark   (den)

4. hot land   (bats)

5. later in the day   (dry)

6. where skunks sleep   (morning)

7. not wet   (night)

8. a cool place   (desert)

                                             (little)

C Put a ✔ by the words that tell <u>where</u>. Put an X by the words that tell <u>when</u>.

1. _____ in the morning

2. _____ under a rock

3. _____ in the shade

4. _____ at night

5. _____ in a den

6. _____ in the afternoon

7. _____ on the sand

8. _____ in the daytime

D Write the word to finish the sentence. Use these words.

cool	den	water	shade	snake

_____

1. The desert is _____ at night.

_____

2. Foxes sleep in a _____.

_____

3. Lizards drink _____.

_____

4. Lizards spend the day in the _____.

141

Name _____ Date _____

E You read two selections about deserts. Put a ✔ by sentences that tell about <u>both</u> selections.

1. _____ They tell about deserts.

2. _____ They tell about a cactus.

3. _____ They tell about dens.

4. _____ They tell how animals live in deserts.

5. _____ They tell when animals sleep.

6. _____ They tell about camels.

7. _____ They tell when animals look for food.

8. _____ They show pictures of desert animals.

9. _____ They tell about special parts.

10. _____ They tell why it is hard to live in the desert.

F Circle the animals that are in <u>both</u> selections.

lizard	camel	fox	skunk
bat	snake	owl	rabbit

G Tell how the pictures in the two selections are different.

_____

_____

_____

_____

_____

Selection 34: Paired
Core Skills Reading Comprehension, Grade 1

Skills Review: Selections 27–34

A Four leaves are on each tree. Put the number of each word on the right tree. The first one is done for you.

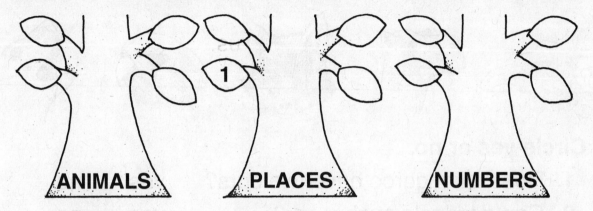

ANIMALS

1. sea
2. kangaroo
3. pond
4. camel

PLACES

5. five
6. eight
7. six
8. seal

NUMBERS

9. desert
10. ten
11. bird
12. doghouse

B Draw lines to match these.

1. to pick up

2. to get to it

3. not as long

4. one who works with you

5. up to the time of

6. made a dog noise

7. a baby frog

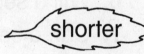 shorter

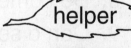 helper

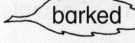 barked

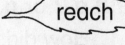 reach

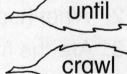 until

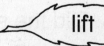 crawl

lift

 tadpole

Name _____ Date _____

C **What do you know about foxes and seals?**

1. Circle the fox's nose.
2. Put a ✔ on the seal's nose.

D **Circle yes or no.**

1. Does a kangaroo have two ears?	yes	no
2. Can a tadpole push a car?	yes	no
3. Will a fox eat a bird?	yes	no
4. Do giraffes have wings?	yes	no
5. Do giraffes have long necks?	yes	no
6. Will a seal eat a fish?	yes	no
7. Can a seal fly?	yes	no
8. Do camels live in the desert?	yes	no
9. Can a seal swim?	yes	no
10. Do seals read fast?	yes	no

E **Put a ? or a . at the end of each sentence.**

1. How did the purple flower get there
2. What hopped on two big back feet
3. Are the front legs shorter
4. Ray found his lunchbox at school
5. Did the seals eat many fish
6. Baby Seal could smell his mother
7. The giraffe reaches leaves with its long neck

144

Name _____ Date _____

F **Can you do this?**

1. Color six flowers purple.
   Color the other one red.

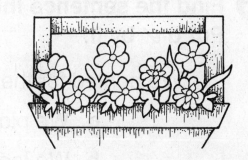

2. Here is Ray's coat.
   Put four green buttons on it.

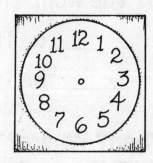

3. Sara and Dad worked
   until five o'clock.
   Show this time on
   the clock.

4. Here is what Rosa saw.
   Put an **X** on what came
   out of the eggs. Circle
   the mother animal.

5. Mother Fox and her
   little foxes are
   looking for food.
   Color the two little
   foxes brown. Color
   Mother Fox red.

Skills Review: Selections 27–34
Core Skills Reading Comprehension, Grade 1

G Find the sentence that means the same as the first one. Put a ✔ by it.

1. We hunted for the toy.

_____ **a.** We played with the toy.

_____ **b.** We looked for the toy.

2. Rosa is shorter than Roy.

_____ **a.** Rosa is not as tall as Roy.

_____ **b.** Rosa is bigger than Roy.

3. The worm crawled to the rock.

_____ **a.** The worm reached the rock.

_____ **b.** The worm dropped the rock.

H When? Where? Put the words that tell <u>when</u> in the <u>WHEN?</u> box. Put the words that tell <u>where</u> in the <u>WHERE?</u> box. Draw lines to the right box.

1. at school

2. in the pond

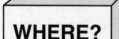
WHEN?

3. long ago

4. in the afternoon

WHERE?

5. now

6. on the sofa

7. one day

8. next to me

9. after lunch

10. by the sea

Answer Key

Selection 1
pages 1–3

A 1. dog
   2. Tags
   3. people
   4. big dog
   5. The people walk.
   6. a big house

B 1. Pictures b, c, d
   2. Pictures a, d

Selection 2
pages 4–6

A 2. yes   5. no
   3. no   6. yes
   4. yes   7. no

B 1. Here is a big animal.
   2. Animals run here.
   3. See people here.
   4. Here is a new cat.
   5. A dog is in the house.
   6. No cat is here.

Selection 3
pages 7–9

A Pictures 1, 3, 4, 5

B 1. Children get food.
   2. People live here.
   3. Here is food.
   4. Children see food.
   5. The people work here.
   6. People get food.

Selection 4
pages 10–12

A 2. food   5. homes
   3. work   6. working
   4. house   7. here

B 2. Picture b
   3. Picture b
   4. Picture a

Skills Review: Selections 1–4
pages 13–14

A 1. new
   2. not new
   3. is not working
   4. can get food
   5. The house is not new.
   6. People work here.

B 1. walk   5. food
   2. home   6. working
   3. here   7. people
   4. new

Selection 5
pages 15–17

A 2. yes   5. no
   3. yes   6. yes
   4. yes   7. yes

B house: birdhouse, cabin, house
   food: eggs, fruit
   people: woodchopper, firefighters

Selection 6
pages 18–20

A 1. man with hammer
   2. rock
   3. Dad
   4. spider
   5. Mom
   6. children and Dad
   7. Mom and Dad
   8. house

B Row 1: Dan, Will
   Row 2: Mom, Dad
   Row 3: Nan
   Row 4: children
   Row 5: Jill

C 1. cannot walk
   2. are in a house
   3. can eat
   4. is new

Selection 7
pages 21–23

A 2. The Raccoon's Home

B 1. Food for People
   2. The Raccoons Get Food

C 1. no   5. no
   2. yes   6. yes
   3. yes   7. no
   4. yes

Selection 8
pages 24–26

A Picture 1: 3, 4
   Picture 2: 1, 3
   Picture 3: 1, 4
   Picture 4: 3, 4
   Picture 5: 3, 4

B 1. no   5. no
   2. yes   6. yes
   3. yes   7. no
   4. no

Selection 9
pages 27–29

A 1. fish/brook
   2. ant/anthill
   3. bee/beehive
   4. raccoon/tree
   5. girl/house

B 1. flowers   5. good
   2. something 6. it
   3. home   7. eat
   4. food

147

Skills Review: Selections 5–9
pages 30–32

A 1. lion
   2. bees
   3. hills
   4. make a new house
   5. bugs and flowers

B Selection 1: 2.
What Animals Eat
Selection 2: 3.
Something for Mom

C Picture 1: 2, 3
Picture 2: 1, 3

Selection 10
pages 33–35

A Picture 1: bird, squirrel, raccoon
Picture 2: people, children

B 1. yes   6. yes
   2. no   7. no
   3. no   8. yes
   4. yes   9. no
   5. yes   10. yes

Selection 11
pages 36–38

A 2. b   4. c
   3. b   5. a

B 1. e
   2. c
   3. a
   4. b

Selection 12
pages 39–41

A 2. Picture b
   3. Picture a
   4. Picture b
   5. Picture b

B 1. ant   5. bee
   2. bird   6. people
   3. corn   7. ant
   4. duck

Selection 13
pages 42–44

A 1. a   4. a
   2. b   5. b
   3. b   6. a

B 1. bugs   4. play
   2. fish   5. swim
   3. hill

Skills Review: Selections 10–13
pages 45–47

A 1. grass   4. flower
   2. raccoon   5. duck
   3. frog   6. fish

B Selection 1: 3. The Animals
Have Fun
Selection 2: 1. The Fox Will Not
Eat a Frog

C 1. fun   4. bugs
   2. corn   5. you
   3. swim

Selection 14: Paired
pages 48–50

A 1. c. get food
   2. b. "I will not eat a
       chipmunk."

B 1. ground
   2. run
   3. lives

C 1. on the ground
   2. happy people
   3. two rocks
   4. a frog by a flower
   5. on the grass
   6. is a bird

Selection 15: Paired
pages 51–54

A 2. A Snake in the House

B 1. fast
   2. door
   3. rocks

C 3, 1, 2

D 2. c   4. a
   3. a   5. c

E 1. a
   2. a
   3. b
   4. c

Selection 16
pages 55–57

A 1. c
   2. b

B 1. on a squirrel
   2. on a raccoon
   3. under a flower
   4. on the hill
   5. in a spider's home
   6. on the corn

C 1. gorilla   3. jacket
   2. corn   4. ladder

D Discuss children's answers.

Skills Review: Selections 14–16
pages 58–61

A 2. b
   3. a
   4. b

B 1. mud   5. a door
   2. away   6. a hill
   3. people   7. bugs
   4. a snake

C 1. happy
   2. fast
   3. want

D 1. a
   2. b

E 1. The Happy People

F 3, 2, 1

148

Selection 17
pages 62–65

A 2. a   5. b
    3. b   6. c
    4. c

B 2. new   5. finger
    3. hop   6. paws
    4. back

C 2. back   5. paw
    3. tail   6. pouch
    4. front

D 2. It   5. He
    3. She   6. They
    4. It   7. It

Selection 18
pages 66–69

A 1. b   4. c
    2. b   5. b
    3. b   6. b

B 1. mud   5. tail
    2. tub   6. back
    3. morning   7. fun
    4. happy

C 1. c
    2. b
    3. a

D 1. it   4. it
    2. them   5. She
    3. They

E Correct order: 1, 3, 2

Selection 19
pages 70–73

A 2. b   4. c
    3. a   5. c

B 2. food   5. fun
    3. swim   6. walk
    4. pond

C 1. c   4. a
    2. no picture   5. d
    3. b

D 1. two
    2. one

E Correct order: 2, 3, 1

Selection 20
pages 74–77

A 1. c   5. b
    2. b   6. c
    3. c   7. b
    4. a   8. b

B 2. morning   6. blue
    3. robin   7. father
    4. mother   8. nest
    5. oak

C 1. c   4. b
    2. no picture   5. a
    3. d

D 1. them   4. it
    2. They   5. Her
    3. him

E 1. yes
    2. no
    3. yes

Selection 21
pages 78–81

A 1. a   5. b
    2. b   6. a
    3. c   7. c
    4. c

B 2. forgot   6. children
    3. lettuce   7. afternoon
    4. milk   8. corner
    5. money

C 2. house   4. girl
    3. walk   5. black

D 1. Andy
    2. Mom
    3. Ann

E Correct order: 2, 1, 3

Skills Review : Selections 17–21
pages 82–85

A 1. four   5. four
    2. zero   6. zero
    3. zero   7. four
    4. four   8. zero

B 1. He
    2. them
    3. They

C 1. pouch   5. park
    2. food   6. night
    3. afternoon   7. front
    4. again

D 1. a
    2. b
    3. b

E 1. hop   5. back
    2. grass, mud   6. money
    3. tub   7. grass
    4. forgot

F Correct order: 3, 1, 2

G 1. b
    2. a
    3. e
    4. f
    5. d

Selection 22
pages 86–89

A 1. c   5. a
    2. b   6. b
    3. c   7. b
    4. b

B 1. seven   6. shelf
    2. bottom   7. every
    3. Sunday   8. toys
    4. evening   9. middle
    5. eight

C Children color and place objects on shelves as directed.

D 1. top   4. play
    2. top   5. care
    3. play   6. care

E 1. Bill   4. Bob
    2. Bev   5. Bev
    3. Bob   6. Bev

Selection 23
pages 90–93

A 1. c   5. a
     2. c   6. a
     3. b   7. c
     4. a

B 1. c   6. yes
     2. no   7. no
     3. no   8. yes
     4. yes   9. yes
     5. no

C 1. bug
     2. fox

D 2. out   5. stop
     3. down   6. little
     4. off   7. bad

E 1. Circle 4.
     2. Rabbit's House
     3. no

Selection 24
pages 94–97

A 1. b   6. a
     2. a   7. b
     3. c   8. b
     4. c   9. c
     5. c   10. c

B 1. hopped
     2. tiger
     3. green
     4. left
     5. tall
     6. hunt
     7. quick

C 4, 5, 6, 8, 9

D 1. a
     2. c
     3. a

Selection 25
pages 98–101

A 1. May   3. Rita
     2. Jeff   4. Ted

B 1. c   6. c
     2. a   7. a
     3. a   8. c
     4. c   9. b
     5. b

C 1. hurry   7. Monday
     2. shoe   8. ready
     3. school   9. last
     4. second   10. playground
     5. watched   11. race
     6. started

D 1. start   3. runners
     2. winner   4. run

E 1. 8
Color the flags in this order:
blue, green, red, red, red, red,
brown, yellow. Circle the
brown flag.

Selection 26
pages 102–105

A 1. a   5. c
     2. b   6. c
     3. c   7. b
     4. b

B 1. less   5. white
     2. mittens   6. Thursday
     3. lost   7. money
     4. snow

C 1. c
     2. b

D 1. Sunday
     2. Monday
     3. Tuesday
     4. Wednesda
     5. Thursday
     6. Friday
     7. Saturday

E 1. b
     2. c
     3. b

Skills Review: Selections 22–26
pages 106–109

A 1. d   4. a
     2. g   5. c
     3. b

B Colors: yellow, white, green
Numbers: eight, seven, nine
Animals: tiger, worm, duck

C 1. less   5. evening
     2. hunt   6. last
     3. second   7. quick
     4. left   8. every

D 1. hill   4. fish
     2. snow   5. worm
     3. water   6. tiger

E Put an X on the middle book,
color the top book green, color
the bottom book orange, make
a brown hole in bottom of the
shoe, and color the shoe yellow.

F 1. left   3. last
     2. left   4. last

G 1. Put an X on 3.
     2. Underline *The Ice Melts*.
     3. Circle 6.

Selection 27
pages 110–113

A 1. c   4. b
     2. c   5. c
     3. b   6. a

B 1. spring   5. purple
     2. window   6. plant
     3. never   7. surprise
     4. found

C 1. up   4. there
     2. came   5. never
     3. drop

D 1. .   4. .
     2. ?   5. .
     3. ?   6. ?

E 1. Every flower they planted
was red.
     2. Little green plants came up
before the flowers.
     3. They did not know the purple
flower was there.

150

Selection 28
pages 114–117

A
1. c   5. c
2. c   6. b
3. a   7. b
4. b   8. c

B
1. c   4. a or e
2. d   5. b
3. a or e

C
1. They had one girl and two boys.
2. He came out of the school at noon.
3. They lost the book one more time.

D
1. three   4. let's
2. Mr.   5. lunch
3. lost   6. button

E Where: 2, 3, 6, 7
When: 1, 4, 5, 8

Selection 29
pages 118–121

A
1. b   4. b
2. a   5. c
3. b   6. a

B
1. pup   5. baby
2. mother   6. barked
3. rock   7. swim
4. gone   8. smell

C
1. ?   5. .
2. ?   6. ?
3. .   7. ?
4. ?   8. ?

D
2. c   7. c
3. a   8. b
4. a   9. c
5. b   10. a
6. c

Selection 30
pages 122–125

A
1. a   5. b
2. a   6. c
3. c   7. b
4. c

B
1. jar   4. tails
2. front   5. shorter
3. legs   6. jelly

C Check ✔ 2, 5, 8.
Mark X on 1, 3, 4, 6, 7.

D
1. b   3. b
2. c   4. c

Selection 31
pages 126–129

A
1. b   4. c
2. a   5. c
3. a   6. b

B
1. near   6. wish
2. grab   7. until
3. nothing   8. wings
4. pond   9. land
5. foxes

C
1. ?   6. .
2. .   7. ?
3. .   8. ?
4. ?   9. ?
5. ?

D
1. b
2. b

E
1. c
2. b
3. a

Selection 32
pages 130–133

A
1. b   4. c
2. a   5. b
3. b

B
1. reach   6. lifted
2. tiny   7. watch
3. mouth   8. wings
4. grab   9. neck
5. crawl   10. drink

C
1. plants   3. meat
2. plants   4. meat

D
1. b
2. b
3. b

E Check ✔ 2, 4, 5, 8.
Mark X on 1, 3, 6, 7.

Selection 33: Paired
pages 134–137

A
1. a   4. c
2. b   5. b
3. a

B
1. camel   4. desert
2. dry   5. little
3. cactus

C
1. c
2. a
3. d
4. b

D
1. cactus
2. camel

E
1. sand   3. parts
2. skin   4. night

151

Selection 34: Paired
pages 138–141

A 1. c   **5.** b
    2. b   **6.** c
    3. a   **7.** b
    4. b   **8.** c

B **2.** bats
    3. night
    4. desert
    5. afternoon
    6. den
    7. dry
    8. shade

C Check ✔ 2, 3, 5, 7.
Mark X on 1, 4, 6, 8.

D **1.** cool
    2. den
    3. water
    4. shade

E Check ✔ 1, 4, 5, 7, 8, 10.

F lizard, snake

G Possible response: The selection
33 picture has words.

Skills Review: Selections 27–34
pages 143–146

A Animals: 2, 4, 8, 11
Places: 1, 3, 9, 12
Numbers: 5, 6, 7, 10

B **1.** lift   **5.** until
    2. reach   **6.** barked
    3. shorter   **7.** tadpole
    4. helper

C **1.** Circle the fox's nose.
    2. Check ✔ the seal's nose.

D **1.** yes   **6.** yes
    2. no   **7.** no
    3. yes   **8.** yes
    4. no   **9.** yes
    5. yes   **10.** no

E **1.** ?   **5.** ?
    2. ?   **6.** .
    3. ?   **7.** .
    4. .

F **1.** Color 6 flowers purple and
one flower red.
    2. Add 4 green buttons to
the coat.
    3. Draw hands to show
5 o'clock.
    4. Put Xs on 3 tadpoles and
circle the frog.
    5. Color the little foxes brown
and the Mother Fox red.

G **1.** b
    2. a
    3. a

H When: 3, 4, 5, 7, 9
Where: 1, 2, 6, 8, 10

152